# A DIGEST OF

# SUPREME COURT DECISIONS

# AFFECTING EDUCATION

PERRY A. ZIRKEL, EDITOR

PHI DELTA KAPPA
Bloomington, Indiana

ISBN 0-87367-764-1

Library of Congress Catalog Card Number 78-53582

To Lou and Helen
with love

# Phi Delta Kappa Commission on the Impact of Court Decisions on Education

Perry A. Zirkel, Chairperson

Dean and Professor
School of Education
Lehigh University

David G. Carter

Associate Dean and
Associate Professor
School of Education
University of Connecticut

Gene V Glass

Professor of Educational Research
University of Colorado

Henry S. Lufler, Jr.

Assistant Dean
School of Education
University of Wisconsin

Marion A. McGhehey

Executive Secretary
National Organization on Legal
Problems of Education

Robert E. Phay

Professor of Public Law
and Government
University of North Carolina

Philip K. Piele

Associate Professor and Director,
ERIC Clearinghouse on Educational
Management
University of Oregon

Bernard H. Shulman

Superintendent of Schools
Canton, Massachusetts

Robert J. Nearine, Evaluator

Director of Evaluation
Hartford, Connecticut
Board of Education

Lowell C. Rose, PDK Liaison

Executive Secretary
Phi Delta Kappa International

# ACKNOWLEDGMENTS

The Commission acknowledges its appreciation for the support and cooperation of Phi Delta Kappa under the able leadership of Lowell C. Rose, Executive Secretary.

The principal research assistance for this volume was provided by Deborah Green, an attorney in Connecticut. Attorney Lorenzo Smith and law students Harry Franklin and Michael Jainchill also assisted in the preparation of this material.

The reviewers for the various chapters were Philip K. Piele (School District Finance and Organization), Marion A. McGhehey (Church-State Relationships in Education), Henry S. Lufler, Jr. and Michael Roth (Student Rights and Responsibilities), Bernard H. Shulman (Employee Rights and Responsibilities), David G. Carter (Race, Language, and Sex Discrimination), Aviam Soifer and Perry Zirkel (Procedural Parameters). Professor Soifer also assisted in the preparation of the Glossary. Martha McCarthy of Indiana University provided a final review of the entire digest.

The Commission also expresses its appreciation to Rita Costantino and Marcia Berkow who patiently typed the successive drafts of the digest.

# Introduction

This digest is a product of the Phi Delta Kappa Commission on the Impact of Court Decisions on Education. It is designed to serve as a ready reference tool for practitioners and others interested in school law. The scope of the digest is limited to U. S. Supreme Court cases because of their pervasive impact. It is not the intent of this digest to be a complete compilation of case law affecting education. Many important decisions affecting school policies and practices are handed down by state courts, e.g., regarding school finance reform; and lower federal courts, e.g., concerning student rights. Thus, readers are encouraged to become familiar also with the respective state court rulings as well as state statutes and administrative regulations in their jurisdiction. Furthermore, this digest is intended to serve as a supplement to, not a substitute for, reading the Supreme Court cases themselves, studying written interpretations of them, and consulting competent counsel.

## Content

The principal source material for this digest consists of Supreme Court decisions directly affecting students and staff in kindergarten through grade twelve. Older and overruled cases, e.g., *Plessy* and *Gobitis* are included for their historical importance. In addition, a few cases in higher education, e.g., *Healy* and *Roemer*, and juvenile law, e.g., *In re Gault*, are included to provide perspective of these related areas of the law that are relevant to, but not identical to, the K-12 school context. Finally, decisions involving nonschool litigants are included insofar as they have direct impact on students or staff. In the Table of Contents the categories of litigants are coded to the right of the case names as follows: 1. public school litigants, 2. private school litigants, 3. higher education litigants, 4. nonschool litigants.

The case entries are organized into five substantive chapters and one procedural chapter. This latter chapter is included to illustrate procedural hurdles that can cause the substantive issues posed in a case to go unresolved. Cross references are provided in the Table of Contents for cases that fit more than one chapter heading. The Table of Contents also indicates summary affirmances (see the Glossary) and one-judge opinions in chambers (see the desegregation decisions in Chapter V) as well as those decisions in which the Court has rendered a full opinion on the merits.

The digest includes cases decided by the Court as of July 1977. It is anticipated that decisions after this date will be included in periodic supplements to the digest. The digest does not include cases in which the Supreme Court has denied certiorari (see the Glossary). Also, constitutional, statutory, and administrative sources of law are omitted except insofar as they are incorporated in the Supreme Court decisions.

*Format*

The entry for each case includes the following information: 1. the citation, 2. the facts, 3. the holding, and 4. the basis for the decision. The citations follow the style of the Harvard Law Review Association, *A Uniform System of Citation*, 12th ed. (1976). The volume number and that of the first page of the case as it appears in the official reports of the Supreme Court are given except where only an unofficial report of the decision ("S.Ct." for West's *Supreme Court Reporter* and "U.S.L.W." for *United States Law Week*) was available at the time of the preparation of this digest in July 1977. The lower court history of the decisions is not listed except in cases resulting in a summary disposition, i.e., summary affirmance, dismissal, etc. For the typical case, the form of the citation is summarized below:

SPRINGFIELD v. QUICK,    63       U.S.       56       (1859)
   (appellant)   (appellee) (vol.#) (U.S. Reports) (page #) (year of decision)

The facts for each decision are presented as much as possible in lay language. For instance, even such common legal terms as "plaintiff" and "appellant" are generally not used in each entry. Since a limited amount of technical language cannot be avoided, a glossary is provided at the end of the volume. For the sake of brevity, facts not essential to the decision are not included in the summary. The "holding," like the "facts," is extrapolated from the majority opinion of the Court except for summary dispositions, in which instances the facts and decision of the lower court are summarized (see the explanation under summary affirmance in the Glossary). The vote of the Court is reported as follows: number of justices in the majority, number in the concurrence, followed by the number dissenting, indicated for example by (5/2 x 2). The numbers are arbitrarily listed as one-half in some cases as an approximate indication of split votes as follows: (5/2½ x1½).

The basis for each decision is listed in terms of the constitutional precedents, statutory sections, or judicial precedents cited by the Court as its primary authority. Legal reasoning is presented only to the extent it helps establish the authority for the decisions. Cases resulting in a summary disposition serve again as an exception. The basis for such cases is given, in the absence of a readily available alternative, in terms of the lower court's opinion. Dismissals and vacated opinions, which are limited to the Procedural Parameters chapter, are dealt with in terms of an explanation of the Court's ruling.

Because they are frequently referred to in the cases, selected federal constitutional provisions are cited below:

**Article I, section 8:**

General Welfare Clause — "The Congress shall have the Power To . . . provide for the . . . general Welfare of the United States . . . . "

Commerce Clause — "To regulate Commerce . . . among the several states . . . . "

**Article I, section 10:**

Impairment of Contracts Clause — "No State shall . . . pass any Bill of Attainder, ex post facto Law, or Law impairing the Obligation of Contracts . . . . "

**Article III:** — "The judicial Power shall extend to all Cases, in Law and Equity, arising under this Constitution, the Laws of the United States, and Treaties [etc.] . . . to Controversies . . . between Citizens of different States; [etc.] . . . "

**Amendment I:**

Establishment and Free Exercise Clauses — "Congress shall make no law respecting an establishment of religion, or prohibiting the free exercise thereof . . . . "

Freedom of Expression Clause — "Or abridging the freedom of speech . . . . "

Freedom of Assembly Clause — "Or the right of the people peaceably to assemble . . . . "

**Amendment V:**

Due Process Clause (Congress) — "No person shall be . . . deprived of life, liberty, or property without due process of law . . . . "

Self-Incrimination Clause — "nor shall be compelled in any criminal case to be a witness against himself . . . . "

**Amendment VIII:** — "[N] or cruel and unusual punishment inflicted . . . . "

| | |
|---|---|
| **Amendment X:** | "The powers not delegated to the United States by the Constitution, nor prohibited by it to the States, are reserved to the States . . . . " |
| **Amendment XI:** | "The Judicial power of the United States shall not . . . extend to any suit in law or equity, . . . against one of the United States by Citizens of another State . . . . " |
| **Amendment XIII:** | "Neither slavery nor involuntary servitude, except as a punishment for crime . . . shall exist within the United States . . . . " |
| **Amendment XIV:** | |
| Due Process Clause (States) | "[N] or shall any State deprive any person of life, liberty, or property, without due process of law . . . . " |
| Equal Protection Clause | "nor deny to any person within its jurisdiction the equal protection of the laws . . . . " |

This digest is designed to fill a gap in the legal literature and knowledge of educators. It is hoped that its simplicity of presentation, augmented by the prudence of its readers, will clarify Supreme Court decisions that affect education.

Bethlehem, Pennsylvania
December 1977

Perry A. Zirkel

# Table of Contents

*Page*

iii  Dedication
v  Acknowledgments
vi  Introduction

1 — **Chapter I.  School District Finance And Organization**

2 —  Springfield v. Quick                                            1
3 —  Davis v. Indiana                                                1
3 —  Doon v. Cummins                                                 1
4 —  Atchison Board of Education v. DeKay                            1
5 —  Indiana *ex rel.* Stanton v. Glover                             1
6 —  New Orleans v. Fisher                                           1
6 —  Attorney General of Michigan *ex rel.* Kies v. Lowrey          1
7 —  Montana *ex rel.* Haire v. Rice                                 1
8 —  Sailors v. Board of Education                                   1
9 —  McInnis v. Ogilvie                                           *  1
9 —  Kramer v. Union Free School District No. 15                     1
10 —  Turner v. Fouche                                               1
11 —  Hadley v. Junior College District                             3
12 —  Askew v. Hargrave                                              1
13 —  Gordon v. Lance                                                1
115 —  Johnson v. New York State Education Department                1  (cr)
13 —  San Antonio Independent School District
                    v. Rodriguez                                     1

---

Explanation of symbols in the Table of Contents

    \* summary affirmance
  \*\* one-judge opinion in chambers
   1 public education, grades K-12
   2 private or parochial education, grades K-12
   3 higher education
   4 other
(cr) cross reference

49433

15 — **Chapter II.   Church-State Relationships In Education**

16 — Pierce v. Society of Sisters                                    2
16 — Cochran v. Louisiana State Board of Education                   2
35 — Minersville School District v. Gobitis                          1   (cr)
36 — Taylor v. Mississippi                                           4   (cr)
17 — Everson v. Board of Education                                   2
18 — Illinois *ex rel.* McCollum v. Board of Education               1
113 — Doremus v. Board of Education                                  1   (cr)
18 — Zorach v. Clauson                                               1
19 — Engel v. Vitale                                                 1
19 — Abington School District v. Schempp,
            Murray v. Curlett                                        1
20 — Chamberlin v. Dade County Board of
            Public Instruction                                      1
114 — Flast v. Cohen                                                 2   (cr)
20 — Board of Education v. Allen                                     2
61 — Epperson v. Arkansas                                            1   (cr)
21 — Walz v. Tax Commission                                          4
21 — Lemon v. Kurtzman, Earley v. Dicenso ("Lemon I")               2
23 — Johnson v. Sanders                                            * 2
24 — Wisconsin v. Yoder                                              1
24 — Lemon v. Kurtzman ("Lemon II")                                 2
25 — Levitt v. Commission for Public Education
            and Religious Liberty                                   2
26 — Committee for Public Education and
            Religious Liberty v. Nyquist                            2
27 — Sloan v. Lemon                                                 2
27 — Wheeler v. Barrera                                             2
28 — Meek v. Pittenger                                              2
118 — Citizens for Parental Rights v. San Mateo County
            Board of Education                                      1   (cr)
29 — Roemer v. Board of Public Works                               3
30 — Wolman V. Walter                                              2

32 — **Chapter III. Student Rights And Responsibilities**

33 — Jacobson v. Massachusetts                                      4
34 — Waugh v. Board of Trustees                                     3
35 — Zucht v. King                                                  1
35 — Minersville School District v. Gobitis                         1
36 — Taylor v. Mississippi                                          4

36 — West Virginia State Board of Education v. Barnette      1

37 — *In re* Gault      4

38 — Tinker v. Des Moines Independent
Community School District      1

38 — Police Department v. Mosley      1

39 — Grayned v. City of Rockford      1

41 — Healy v. James      3

42 — Papish v. Board of Curators      3

42 — Goss v. Lopez      1

117 — Board of School Commissioners v. Jacobs      1    (cr)

43 — Wood v. Strickland      1

45 — Baker v. Owen      * 1

46 — Ingraham v. Wright      1

## 47 — Chapter IV. Employee Rights And Responsibilities

48 — Meyer v. Nebraska      2

49 — Bartels v. Iowa      2

49 — Phelps v. Board of Education      1

50 — Dodge v. Board of Education      1

50 — Indiana *ex rel.* Anderson v. Brand      1

51 — Garner v. Board of Public Works      4

52 — Adler v. Board of Education      1

53 — Wieman v. Updegraff      3

54 — Slochower v. Board of Higher Education      3

54 — Beilan v. Board of Public Education      1

55 — Lerner v. Casey      4

56 — Shelton v. Tucker      1

56 — Cramp v. Board of Public Instruction      1

57 — Baggett v. Bullitt      3

58 — Elfbrandt v. Russell      1

58 — Keyishian v. Board of Regents      3

59 — Whitehill v. Elkins      3

60 — Pickering v. Board of Education      1

60 — Maryland v. Wirtz      4

61 — Epperson v. Arkansas      1

62 — Connell v. Higginbotham      1

62 — Cole v. Richardson      4

63 — Board of Regents v. Roth      3

64 — Perry v. Sindermann      3

65 — Geduldig v. Aiello      3

98 — Cleveland Board of Education v. LaFleur,
  Cohen v. Chesterfield County School Board     1   (cr)

116 — Mercer v. Michigan State Board of Education     *   1   (cr)

66 — McCarthy v. Philadelphia Civil Service Commission     4

66 — Bishop v. Wood     4

67 — Hortonville Joint School District No. 1
  v. Hortonville Education Association     1

68 — National League of Cities v. Usery     4

68 — Massachusetts Board of Retirement v.
  Murgia     4

69 — Madison v. Wisconsin Employment Relations
  Commission     1

70 — Mount Healthy City School District v. Doyle     1

71 — Codd v. Velger     4

72 — Abood v. Detroit Board of Education     1

72 — International Brotherhood of Teamsters
  v. United States     4

## 74 — Chapter V.   Race, Language, And Sex Discrimination

76 — Plessy v. Ferguson     4

77 — Cumming v. Richmond County Board of Education     1

77 — Farrington v. Tokushige     1

78 — Gong Lum v. Rice     1

79 — Sweatt v. Painter     3

79 — McLaurin v. Oklahoma State Regents
  for Higher Education     3

80 — Brown v. Board of Education ("Brown I")     1

81 — Bolling v. Sharpe     1

81 — Brown v. Board of Education ("Brown II")     1

82 — Cooper v. Aaron     1

82 — Goss v. Board of Education     1

83 — Griffin v. County School Board     1

84 — Bradley v. School Board ("Bradley I")     1

84 — Rogers v. Paul     1

85 — Green v. County School Board     1

85 — Monroe v. Board of Commissioners     1

86 — United States v. Montgomery County
  Board of Education     1

87 — Alexander v. Holmes County Board of Education     1

87 — Dowell v. Board of Education     1

88 — Carter v. West Feliciana Parish School Board     1

88 — Griggs v. Duke Power Co.                                      4
89 — Williams v. McNair                                      *    3
90 — Swann v. Charlotte-Mecklenburg Board
        of Education                                               1
91 — Davis v. Board of School Commissioners                       1
92 — McDaniel v. Barresi                                          1
92 — Guey Hung Lee v. Johnson                               **   1
93 — Spencer v. Kugler                                       *   1
93 — Jefferson Parish School Board v. Dandridge              **  1
94 — Wright v. Council of City of Emporia                         1
95 — United States v. Scotland Neck City Board
        of Education                                               1
95 — Drummond v. Acree                                       **  1
96 — Keyes v. School District No. 1, Denver, Colorado             1
97 — Norwood v. Harrison                                          2
98 — Lau v. Nichols                                               1
98 — Cleveland Board of Education v. LaFleur,
        Cohen v. Chesterfield County School Board                 1
99 — Mayor of Philadelphia v. Educational Equality League         1
115 — DeFunis v. Odegaard                                          3    (cr)
100 — Bradley v. School Board ("Bradley II")                       1
65 — Geduldig v. Aiello                                            4    (cr)
101 — Gilmore v. Montgomery                                        4
102 — Milliken v. Bradley ("Milliken I")                           1
103 — Evans v. Buchanan                                      *   1
104 — Washington v. Davis                                          4
105 — Runyon v. McCrary                                            2
105 — Pasadena City Board of Education v. Spangler                 1
106 — Arlington Heights v. Metropolitan
        Housing Development Corp.                                  4
107 — Vorcheimer v. School District of Philadelphia          *   1
108 — Milliken v. Bradley ("Milliken II")                          1
109 — Hazlewood School District v. United States                  1
110 — Dayton Board of Education v. Brinkman                       1

## 112 — Chapter VI.  Procedural Parameters

113 — Doremus v. Board of Education                               1
113 — Ellis v. Dixon                                              1
114 — Flast v. Cohen                                              2
12 — Askew v. Hargrave                                            1    (cr)
115 — Johnson v. New York State Education Department              1

*Page*

115 — DeFunis v. Odegaard                                      3
116 — Mercer v. Michigan State Board of Education        *   1
117 — Board of School Commissioners v. Jacobs               1
118 — Citizens for Parental Rights v. San Mateo County
            Board of Education                                      1
105 — Pasadena City Board of Education v. Spangler          1   (cr)

119 — **Glossary**

123 — **Table of Cases**

128 — **Index**

# I. SCHOOL DISTRICT FINANCE AND ORGANIZATION

*Reviewer:* Philip K. Piele
Associate Professor and Director,
ERIC Clearinghouse on
Educational Management
University of Oregon

What power, consistent with the U.S. Constitution, do state legislatures have to organize and finance public schools within their boundaries? When deciding this question, the U. S. Supreme Court has, with few exceptions, extended broad power to the states under general constitutional construction upholding the state interest in establishing and promulgating free public education for elementary and secondary school-age children. In *Springfield v. Quick*, for example, the court upheld the discretionary power of state legislatures to collect and disburse taxes for educational purposes. And in an equally important school organization case, *Attorney General of Michigan ex rel. Kies v. Lowrey*, the Court unanimously declared that a state legislature has the absolute power to make and change school district boundaries. The Court rejected claims that property rights protected by the due process clause of the Fourteenth Amendment were being infringed. And in *Montana ex. rel. Hair v. Rice*, the Court reaffirmed the discretionary authority of state legislatures to allocate state-acquired funds for the establishment and operation of public schools.

It was not until the late sixties and early seventies that the Supreme Court began a serious re-examination of the constitutional issues related to the organization and finance of public schools in this country. And so far the re-examination has not seriously eroded the broad discretionary power of states to organize and finance public schools. In *McInnis v. Ogilvie*, a precursor to *Rodriguez*, the Court upheld the constitutionality of a state system of funding public schools that relied heavily on the local property tax. The Court declared that the equal protection clause of the Fourteenth Amendment is not applicable where the system of state funding is not arbitrary nor based on invidious discrimination against any identifiable class or group. But in three voter-eligibility and public office-holding cases, *Kramer v. Union Free School District No. 15*, *Turner v. Fouche*, and *Hadley v. Junior College District*, decided in 1969 and 1970, the Court did apply the equal protection clause of

1

the Fourteenth Amendment (1) to declare unconstitutional state voter-eligibility statutes based on ownership of taxable real property and custody of public school children, (2) to strike down public office-holding state statutes based on ownership of property, and (3) to declare unconstitutional a system of trustee apportionment that consistently discriminated in favor of smaller districts. However, in a fourth voting case, *Gordon v. Lance,* the Court declared that a state law requiring a 60% voter approval of bond measures did not violate the equal protection clause of the Fourteenth Amendment because the law did not discriminate against any identifiable class of persons.

And finally, what is perhaps the most significant and certainly the most widely publicized case in this chapter, *San Antonio Independent School District v. Rodriguez,* the Court narrowly (5-4) upheld the constitutionality of a state system of funding public schools based on the local property tax. In finding that the Texas system of financing public education did not violate the equal protection clause, the Court held that there was no "evidence that the [Texas] financing system discriminates against any definable category of 'poor' or that it results in the absolute deprivation of education . . ." Subsequent to this holding by the Court, however, several state supreme courts have declared their state systems of financing public education based on the local property tax to be invalid based on their respective state constitutions.

## SPRINGFIELD v. QUICK, 63 U.S. 56 (1859)

*Facts:* Congress reserved the sixteenth section of the public lands in each township in all new states for the support of public schools within each township. The funds were to be spent only within the township and only for educational purposes.

  The State of Indiana, while maintaining the congressional reservation of each sixteenth section's funds to the educational needs of its township, provided that other sources of school revenue, e.g., those arising from taxes, would be distributed to townships whose sixteenth section funds were less than a per-pupil expenditure allocated by a state program, but that such money would not be allocated to townships whose per-pupil expenditure from sixteenth section funds exceeded this amount. Springfield township, in this latter category, challenged this allocation of state revenues.

*Holding:* (9x0) A state law, that preserves the congressional allocation of sixteenth section funds to each township, but which allocates other state education revenues to townships on the basis of need, is constitutional.

2

*Basis:*     The state legislature has not impinged on the federal government's reservation of sixteenth section funds and has the power to collect and disburse taxes for educational and other purposes at its discretion.

## DAVIS v. INDIANA, 94 U.S. 792 (1876)

*Facts:*     An Act of Congress in admitting Indiana as a state declared that every sixteenth section of a township should be appropriated for the use of schools within the township. A state act directed that the money derived from every sixteenth section of a township should be put into a common fund along with school monies derived from general taxation and should be apportioned among the counties according to the number of pupils in each county. The state act also provided "that in no case shall the congressional township fund be diminished by such distribution, and diverted to any other township." The treasurer of the township refused to pay all the money he received into the common state fund claiming that there was no state law that would permit this money, when paid into the county treasury, to be withdrawn, or if withdrawn, to be applied to the use of schools in the proper congressional township.

*Holding:*     (9x0) Where the school laws of the state do not authorize each county auditor to distribute the school funds in the county treasury to the different townships but do bind him/her not to diminish the school funds, the rights of the inhabitants are sufficiently protected.

*Basis:*     The school treasurer is the very officer who collects and pays money to the fund. The whole fund in the county treasury devoted to the use of schools was to be apportioned and if the fund arising from the sixteenth section becomes a part of it, it also must be distributed. In addition, the statute carefully provides that in making that distribution, the appropriation of the sixteenth section to the schools of the township shall be strictly observed.

## DOON v. CUMMINS, 142 U.S. 366 (1892)

*Facts:*     The 1857 constitution of the State of Iowa provided that "no county, or other political or municipal corporation shall be allowed to become indebted in any manner, or for any purpose,

3

for an amount in the aggregate exceeding 5 percent of the value of taxable property within such county or corporation . . . . " The value of taxable property within the county was a matter of public record ascertainable from the most recent tax lists.

A school district, in order to refinance existing debts, issued bonds in excess of the constitutional limit. These bonds stated on their face that they had been issued in accordance with a state statute authorizing such refinancing. The school district made several interest payments to the buyer and then defaulted on the bonds. In this case, the buyer claims a right to be paid arises from his bond purchase from the school district.

*Holding:*    (6x3) A creditor who lends to a school district an amount in excess of the constitutionally mandated limit on school district indebtedness cannot successfully sue in order to recover such funds, since the constitutional provision prevents the creation of an enforceable debt above the prescribed amount.

*Basis:*    The original buyer of bonds from the school district was charged with the duty of noting the value of taxable property in the district. This amount is a matter of public record. Neither the recitations of legality on the face of the bonds nor the making of interest payments by the school district could create a debt in excess of that permitted in the state constitution.


## ATCHISON BOARD OF EDUCATION v. DEKAY, 148 U. S. 591 (1893)

*Facts:*    As permitted by state law, the school board of Atchison, Kansas, issued bonds with interest coupons attached. The city of Atchison and the Atchison school district had the same geographical boundaries. The bonds were secured by the school fund, which by law was to be raised by the city and by the school property of Atchison, title to which was held by the city. The owner of certain of these bonds brought a suit against the school board for payment due him under the terms of the bonds.

The school board claimed that the bonds were invalid for the following reasons: 1. when naming the statute on authority of which they were issued, the bonds read "an act to organize cities" rather than "incorporate cities" as the act is actually titled; 2. the school board had no right to make the city liable for the bonds and could only attach liability to the school district; and 3. the city council had ratified the bonds when a

4

majority, but not all, of the council members was present and by resolution rather than by ordinance.

The school board also claimed that Atchison's growth in population since the bond issue had made the school board an improper entity to sue. At the time of the bond issuance, the school board was a corporate entity since this was the status of the school boards of class two (smaller) cities under state law. The statutes were silent as to the corporate nature of the school boards of larger cities.

*Holding:* (9x0) (1) Bonds issued by the school board are valid despite misquotation of one word of the title of the enabling statute. (2) The city is properly liable as well as the school district since they are identical in geographic area and are closely linked; indeed, they may be one entity. (3) The bonds are valid despite the fact that only a majority of council members was present when the bonds were ratified. (4) The school board is still a corporate entity although the school boards of class one cities, which Atchison has now become, are not, by statue, corporate entities. Therefore, the bondholder's suit can properly be brought and decided against the school board.

*Bases:* (1) A mere error in copying one word of an enabling statute will not invalidate an otherwise valid document. (2) Under state law at the time of the bond issuance, the school board did not have a corporate identity separate from that of the city and, under the state law, the city was liable for the properly made debts of the school board. (3) The majority of the council's acceptance by resolution of the bond issuance was sufficient and the decision was not required under state law to have been made by an ordinance.

## INDIANA *ex rel.* STANTON v. GLOVER, 155 U.S. 513 (1895)

*Facts:* A creditor sought reinbursement out of a school district trustee's official bond. The trustee had executed and delivered promissory notes for school supplies without first procuring the county commissioners' approval as required by state law. State law also provided that a trustee incurring a debt in a manner contrary to state law was not only liable for his/her bond but also personally liable to the holder of any contract or other evidence of indebtedness for the amount thereof. Finally, state law provided that a trustee had no power to create a debt for school supplies unless supplies suitable and reasonably necessary had actually been delivered to and received by the township. In his law suit the creditor alleged violation of the trustee's obligation to comply with the terms of his employment mandated by state law but did not allege that necessary and suitable school supplies had actually been received by the township. In this case, he challenged the lower court's dismissal of his claim.

*Holding:*　　(9x0) Where a creditor does not allege facts creating an actual debt but only facts indicating a violation of the terms of the school district trustee's employment, he does not have a sufficient claim to reach the trustee's official employment bond.

*Basis:*　　In order for a debt to arise for school supplies state law requires that the supplies be suitable, reasonably necessary, and actually received by the township. Since the creditor did not allege these facts, he did not successfully allege the existence of a debt that could be paid out of the official bond.

## NEW ORLEANS v. FISHER, 180 U.S. 185 (1901)

*Facts:*　　Fisher, a judgment creditor of the board of education, brought an action against the city of New Orleans to recover $10,000 plus interest from the taxes levied for the purpose of paying expenses of the public schools. Fisher alleged that these taxes constituted a trust fund, that the city negligently failed to collect the taxes punctually and also never paid the board of education any interest due on the taxes. The board of education had refused to demand an accounting from the city.

*Holding:*　　(7x0) When a city has collected school taxes and penalties thereon, and has not paid these collections over to the school board, judgment creditors of the board whose claims are payable out of these taxes are entitled to an accounting from the city if the school board refused to demand it.

*Basis:*　　The school taxes collected were held in trust by the city, and the creditors were entitled to the interposition of a court to recheck the fund.

## ATTORNEY GENERAL OF MICHIGAN *ex rel.* KIES v. LOWREY, 199 U.S. 233 (1905)

*Facts:*　　The state constitution requires the legislature to establish and provide a system of public education. In accordance with this requirement the legislature passed laws establishing school districts. In 1881, four school districts were established in the townships of Somerset and Moscow. In 1901, new legislation merged parts of the four original districts to create a new district. This resulted in the old districts losing control over some of the schools they had previously administered and also altered the control of schools within the two townships. In this case, the legislature's power to alter school district boundaries was questioned.

*Holding:*    (9x0) The state legislature has absolute power to make and change the boundaries of subordinate municipalities, including school districts. These governmental sub-divisions cannot claim constitutional protection from alteration by state action.

*Basis:*    The unsuccessful arguments are that the constitutional guarantees of republican government (Article IV) and of the unimpaired right of contract (Article I, section 10) have been violated. Under state law the creation of school districts does not create a contract between such districts and the state. The claim that property rights protected by the Fourteenth Amendment are infringed by the creation of a new district is also rejected.

## MONTANA *ex rel.* HAIRE v. RICE, 204 U.S. 291 (1907)

*Facts:*    An act approved in 1889 admitted several states, including Montana to the Union. The act provided, *inter alia,* (1) that the people of the territory about to become a state would choose delegates to a convention charged with the duty to create a state constitution and government, and (2) that certain lands be given to the State of Montana solely for the support of public schools.

The Montana State Constitution further limited the state legislature's use of such lands by requiring that all assets for the support of schools be invested and that only earned interest be used to pay school costs. In 1905, the state legislature issued bonds. The proceeds from the sale of these bonds were to be used to subsidize an addition to the State Normal School. The bonds were to be secured by proceeds from the sale, lease, or exploitation of the lands that had been granted to Montana by the federal government for the support of the schools.

An architect who had performed valuable services in the construction of the Normal School sought to be paid from the proceeds of the bond issue. The State Treasurer refused to pay, claiming that the bond issue secured by proceeds from the sale or lease of school lands was in violation of the state constitutional requirement that only earned interest be used to support the schools.

Holding: (9x0) A state constitution may properly limit the way in which federal grants of land to the state for the purpose of support of the schools may be used, e.g., it may properly require that such assets not be spent and that only earned interest be expended for the required purpose.

Basis: Where a federal act provides for the establishment of a state constitution and state legislature and also entrusts that legislature with duties and powers, the legislature must, in executing its authority, act in accordance with valid state constitutional limitations on the use of such power.


## SAILORS v. BOARD OF EDUCATION, 387 U.S. 105 (1967)

Facts: In Michigan local school boards are chosen in public elections. Then each local board, without regard to the population of its school district, has an equal voice in the appointment of a five-member county school board which performs functions that are essentially administrative rather than legislative. Voters challenged the constitutionality of this system whereby each local school board, regardless of its district's population, has one vote in the selection of the county board.

Holding: (7/2x0) A system providing for appointment of county school board officials by elected local school board officials is constitutional. There is no requirement that the state provide for the general public election of administrative officials.

Bases: (1) There is no Fourteenth Amendment right to vote for administrative officials. Where there is no right to vote for an official the "one man, one vote" requirement does not obtain. (2) The Court does not decide whether the state may provide for appointment rather than public election of local legislative bodies.

8

## MCINNIS v. SHAPIRO, 293 F. SUPP. 327 (N.D. ILL. 1948), *aff'd sub nom* MCINNIS v. OGILVIE, 394 U.S. 322 (1969)

*Facts:*
The Illinois state system for the funding of public schools is based largely on property taxes. Maximum tax rates and also maximum rates for indebtedness (bond issuance) are set by statute. Variations in tax rates and property value among districts result in a wide variation in district per-pupil expenditures. However, state grants and federal funds assure each district about $400 per pupil and thereby provide a minimum level of education funding. In this case, students from poor districts where per-pupil expenditures are relatively low challenged the state system of school financing.

*Decision:*
Summarily affirmed (8x1)

*Holding:*
(of the three-judge lower court): A state system for funding public schools that relies largely on local property taxation, sets maximum tax rates, and thus mandates wide variation in per-pupil expenditures among districts is constitutional.

*Basis:*
The Fourteenth Amendment, which guarantees due process and equal protection of the law, does not prohibit the state from establishing a rational, decentralized system for funding education based largely on local property taxes. The system is not arbitrary nor is it based on invidious discrimination against a racial, ethnic, or religious group. The system does provide a minimum level of funding to all districts, and there is no constitutional right to an educational funding system based solely on pupil needs or on absolute equality in per-pupil spending.

## KRAMER v. UNION FREE SCHOOL DISTRICT NO. 15, 395 U.S. 621 (1969)

*Facts:*
A bachelor, who neither owned nor leased taxable real property in the district, challenged a New York State statute that prohibited residents, who were otherwise eligible to vote, from voting in school district elections unless they owned or leased taxable real property within the district or had children attending the local public school.

*Holding:*
(6x3) A state statute denying residents of requisite age and citizenship the right to vote in school board elections because

9

they do not own taxable real property in the district or have custody of public school children is unconstitutional.

*Basis:*     The equal protection clause of the Fourteenth Amendment states that no state shall deny persons equal protection of the laws. Where the state is infringing on the right to vote, it must show that there is a compelling state interest; such state interest will be strictly scrutinized by the Court. In this case the Court held that the statute is unconstitutional because the additional voting requirements are broader than necessary in order to limit the pool of voters to those "primarily interested in educational issues." Therefore, the Court did not rule on the issue of whether or not such limitation of the pool of voters is a compelling state interest.

## TURNER v. FOUCHE, 396 U.S. 346 (1970)

*Facts:*     Black residents of Taliaferro County, Georgia, previously brought an action challenging the constitutionality of the system of selection for juries and for school boards. The system in question provided that a county school board of five landowners be selected by a grand jury, which was chosen from the jury list compiled by six jury commissioners. Although the population of Taliaferro County was 60% percent black, all the school board members were white. The trial court had ordered that a new grand jury list be compiled. In so doing, the commissioners, in accordance with their statutory powers, eliminated 178 persons (of whom 171 were black) for not being "upright" and "intelligent." Another 225 persons, many of whom were black, were eliminated because the commissioners were uninformed as to their qualifications. The resulting grand jury list was 37% black. Black residents of the county challenged the trial court's validation of this new grand jury list.

*Holding:*     (9x0) (1) A requirement that members of county boards of education be landonwers is unconstitutional. (2) Where a disproportionate number of blacks are excused from jury lists as being unfit or because those drawing up the list have insufficient information about the members of the black community, either the state must prove there was no racial discrimination or the courts will be constitutionally bound to order corrective measures.

*Bases:*     (1) The equal protection clause of the Fourteenth Amendment does not permit a state to deny the privilege of holding public

10

office to some while extending it to others on the basis of distinctions that violate constitutional guarantees. The requirement that members of the board of education be landowners violates the equal protection clause because there is no rational state interest mandating such a limitation on the privilege of holding public office. (2) While the county system for jury selection does not require racial discrimination and is not unfair as written, its operation is presumed to have been in violation of the Fourteenth Amendment since disproportionate numbers of blacks were eliminated from the jury list. The state offered no explanation to counter the resulting presumption of racial discrimination.

## HADLEY v. JUNIOR COLLEGE DISTRICT, 397 U.S. 50 (1970)

*Facts:*    Missouri law permitted separate school districts to unite to form a consolidated junior college district and then elect six trustees to conduct and manage the district's affairs. The trustees were apportioned among the school districts on the basis of "school enumerations," which are defined as the number of persons from age six through twenty residing in each school district. Within the Kansas City College District, a school district having between 50% and 66 2/3% of the enumeration could elect three, or one-half of the trustees. Similarly, a school district having between 33 1/3% and 50% of the total enumeration could elect two, or one-third of the trustees. One particular school district had 60% of the total college district's "enumeration" but could elect only 50% of the trustees. Residents of the school district challenged the constitutionality of the apportionment of trustees in the Kansas City College District.

*Holding:*    (6x3) When members of an elected body are chosen from separate school districts, the apportionment of members must insure that equal numbers of voters in each district can vote for proportionally equal numbers of officials. A system of trustee apportionment that consistently discriminates in favor of smaller districts is unconstitutional.

*Basis:*    Whenever a state or local government decides to select persons by popular election to perform governmental functions, the equal protection clause of the Fourteenth Amendment requires that each qualified voter have an equal opportunity to participate in that election. In the establishment of voting

11

districts for such elections, the principle of "one man, one vote" must be followed as far as practicable.

## ASKEW v. HARGRAVE, 401 U.S. 476 (1971)

*Facts:* In 1968, Florida enacted a new law concerned with the financing of public education through state funding and local *ad valorem* taxes assessed by each school district. The law provided that a school district must limit *ad valorem* taxes to 10 mills of assessed valuation in order to be eligible to receive state funding. The 10 mill limit was challenged as being discriminatory against school children of property poor districts, since 10 mills would produce less money in those districts. The federal district court invalidated this section of the law on federal constitutional grounds without considering the effect of the entire law on the funding of public education. Before the federal law suit was filed, a state court action challenging the 10 mill limit on state constitutional grounds had been begun.

*Holding:* (per curiam 8/1x10) (1) Federal district courts should not decide federal constitutional questions when the same controversy is challenged in state court on state constitutional grounds. If decided on state constitutional grounds, there would no longer be a need to determine the federal questions involved. (2) Where the effect of an entire funding program on the amount of money available per pupil is crucial to a determination of the federal equal protection issue, the court should not invalidate one section of the new legislation without considering the effect of the entire law.

*Bases:* (1) Where a remedy is available under state law, a federal constitutional claim cannot be decided until the issue of state law has been decided. This policy avoids friction between the states and the federal courts and prevents the unnecessary decision of federal constitutional claims, since a complainant who prevails on state grounds will have no need to pursue a federal claim. (2) The equal protection clause of the Fourteenth Amendment requires that persons not be denied equal protection of the laws. The operation of a law in its entirety must be examined to determine whether it results in a violation of this constitutional mandate.

12

## GORDON v. LANCE, 403 U.S. 1 (1971)

*Facts:*    A West Virginia statute requires a 60% voter approval of measures which add to the public debt or which increase taxation over a certain amount. A proposal calling for the issuance of general obligation bonds was submitted to the voters. By separate ballot, voters were also asked "to authorize the Board of Education to levy additional taxes to support current expenditures and capital improvements." The proposals were defeated because the required 60% voter approval was not attained. Certain voters in favor of the proposals sought to have the 60% rule declared unconstitutional. They claimed that the schools are in great need of improvement, that their level of quality is far below the state average, and that four similar proposals received majority votes but failed due to the 60% rule.

*Holding:*    (6x3) A state law requiring, for bond issue approval or additional taxation, ratification by 60% rather than a simple majority of the voters in a referendum election is constitutional.

*Basis:*    The laws requiring more than a simple majority for ratification of certain questions do not violate the equal protection clause of the Fourteenth Amendment unless the questions singled out for such treatment cause the laws to act unfairly as to any identifiable class of persons. Because the 60% rule in this case applies to all bond issues and taxes for whatever purpose, it does not discriminate against any identifiable class.

## SAN ANTONIO INDEPENDENT SCHOOL DISTRICT v. RODRIGUEZ, 411 U.S. 1 (1973)

*Facts:*    The financing of public elementary and secondary schools in Texas comes from state and local funding. Almost half of the revenues are derived from the state's Minimum Foundation Program which is designed to provide a minimum educational offering in every school in the state. The school districts as a unit provide 20% of the funding for this program. Each district's share is apportioned under a formula designed to reflect its relative tax-paying ability and each district raises these funds by means of a property tax. All districts raise additional monies to support their schools. This revenue source varies with the value of taxable property in the district and results in large disparities in per-pupil spending among districts. In this case, a class representing students who are

13

minority group members or poor and who live in school districts having a low tax base challenged the validity of this funding system. Such a system is widely used in the United States to fund public education.

*Holding:* (5x4) A funding system based on the local property tax that provides a minimum educational offering to all students and that reasonably serves to further the legitimate, state goal of universal, public education is constitutional.

*Basis:* The equal protection clause of the Fourteenth Amendment requires that a strict test of the state law be applied when the law involved operates to the disadvantage of a suspect class of persons or interferes with the exercise of rights and liberties explicitly or implicitly protected by the Constitution. Here, there is no suspect class since students of all incomes and races suffer alike, depending on the tax base of the district in which they attend school. There is no loss of a fundamental right since education, in itself, is not constitutionally protected and since the minimum education guaranteed to every student is sufficient for the exercise of protected political (voting) and First Amendment (expression) rights. Therefore, the financing system must be rationally related merely to a legitimate state purpose to meet the requirements under the Fourteenth Amendment. It is noted that state constitutions may still require stricter standards.

# II. CHURCH-STATE RELATIONSHIPS
# IN EDUCATION

*Reviewer:* Marion A. McGhehey
Executive Secretary
National Organization on
Legal Problems of Education

Cases involving church-state relationships arise primarily out of the First Amendment to the U. S. Constitution which provides that "Congress shall make no law respecting an establishment of religion of prohibiting the free exercise thereof." The prohibitions against Congressional action found in the First Amendment have been applied to the states through the due process clause of the Fourteenth Amendment to the Constitution. Restrictions against state action may be found in state statutes; rules and regulations of the state education agency; policies, rules, and regulations of local school districts; and the actions of school personnel taken under color of state laws.

The first phrase of the First Amendment is customarily called the "establishment" clause. Two types of classifications of cases fall within the establishment classification: cases involving the activity of states in promoting religion through religious practices such as prayer of Bible reading, and cases involving the use of tax revenue to aid church-related institutions.

Bible reading and the use of the Lord's Prayer were held unconstitutional in *Abington* v. *Schempp* and related cases. Released time programs for religious instruction on school premises was held unconstitutional in *McCollum*, but released time where the program itself was conducted away from the school was upheld in *Zorach v. Clauson*. The Court found unconstitutional an Arkansas statute which prohibited teachers in state-supported schools from teaching the Darwinian theory of the evolution of man in *Epperson v. Arkansas.*

While state tax revenue aid which tended to benefit the child rather than the sectarian institution has been upheld as to textbooks in *Cochran* and pupil transportation in *Everson,* more direct forms of aid have been un-constitutional. The loan of textbooks to parochial schools was upheld in the *Allen* and in *Meek* v. *Pittenger* cases, but salary supplements and other forms of direct aid for the payment of the salaries of teachers in parochial schools was held unconstitutional in related cases. Tuition reimbursements and income tax credits to parents of nonpublic school children were found unconstitutional in *Nyquist* and *Sloan,* as were funds reimbursing nonpublic schools for certain administrative services in *Levitt.*

There are relatively few cases involving the "free exercise clause." The Court upheld the validity of mandatory flag salute in *Gobitis,* only to reverse itself a few years later in *Barnette.*

## PIERCE v. SOCIETY OF SISTERS, 268 U.S. 510 (1925)

*Facts:*      An Oregon law which was to take effect in September, 1926, required all normal children between the ages of eight and sixteen to attend public schools until the completion of the eighth grade. Even before becoming enforceable, the law seriously impaired the operation of sectarian and secular private schools within the state. Its enforcement would perhaps result in the destruction of well-established, private elementary school corporations and would greatly diminish the value of property long held for that purpose. In this case, private school corporations sought a court order restraining enforcement of this law.

*Holding:*      (9x0) The state may reasonably regulate all schools and may require that all children attend some school, but the state may not deny children the right to attend *adequate* private schools and force them to attend only public schools.

*Bases:*      The Fourteenth Amendment protects persons from arbitrary state action impairing life, liberty, or property interests. (1) The act requiring children to attend only public primary schools is not reasonably related to a legitimate state purpose since children could be adequately educated in private, as well as in public, schools. (2) The act unreasonably interferes with the liberty of parents to direct the education of their children. (3) The property interests of the private school corporations are severely threatened by the act's impairment of the liberty of their students and patrons.

## COCHRAN v. LOUISIANA STATE BOARD OF EDUCATION, 281 U.S. 370 (1930)

*Facts:*      A state law required that tax money be spent to supply text books to all school children at no charge. Public and private school students, including students of private, sectarian schools were benefited by the program. Suit was brought by a group of

16

taxpayers in Louisiana to restrain the state board of education from expending funds to purchase school books and to supply them free of charge to the school children of the state, on the grounds that it violated the Constitution.

*Holding:*    (9x0) A state statute providing secular textbooks to school children attending private sectarian schools as well as to those attending public schools is constitutional.

*Basis:*    The Fourteenth Amendment forbids the states from depriving a person of life, liberty or property without due process of law. However, the provision of secular texts to all school children serves a public interest and does not benefit the private interest of church schools or of parents of parochial school students in such a way as to violate the due process clause.

## EVERSON v. BOARD OF EDUCATION, 330 U.S. 1 (1947)

*Facts:*    A New Jersey statute authorized its local school districts to make rules and contracts for the transportation of children to and from schools. Acting in accordance with this statute, a local board of education reimbursed parents of school children for the bus fares of students to and from school. While the statute excluded students of private schools operated for profit, it included children who attended private, sectarian schools. In this case, a taxpayer challenged the constitutionality of such payments made to the parents of children attending these private, sectarian schools.

*Holding:*    (5x4) A law authorizing reimbursement of the parents of school children for the bus fares of their children to and from private, sectarian schools, when included in a general program of reimbursement for the bus fares of public school children, is constitutional.

*Bases:*    (1) The due process clause of the Fourteenth Amendment forbids state action which deprives persons of life, liberty, or property without due process of law. However, the claim that reimbursement for bus fares taxes the public in order to serve the private desires of those sending their children to private, sectarian schools, and is therefore prohibited by the Fourteenth Amendment, is without merit. The state can properly decide that the safe transportation of all school children is in the public

17

interest. (2) The establishment clause of the First Amendment, made applicable to the states by the Fourteenth Amendment, prohibits state establishment of religion. However, the provision of governmental services such as police and fire protection, sewage lines and sidewalks, or general reimbursement for school bus fares, without which the church schools would be severely hampered, is viewed by the Court as neutrality toward religion rather than as support of it.

## ILLINOIS *ex rel.* MCCOLLUM v. BOARD OF EDUCATION, 333 U.S. 203 (1948)

*Facts:* An Illinois school board permitted representatives of several religions to teach religion classes to those students in grades four through nine whose parents signed cards indicating that they wanted them to attend. The classes were held during school hours and inside the school building. Students who attended the classes were excused from their secular schedule for that period of time. Other students remained in their regular classes. In this case, a taxpayer challenged the constitutionality of the program.

*Holding:* (3/1/4x1) A program permitting religious instruction within public schools during school hours and excusing students attending such a class from a part of the secular schedule is unconstitutional.

*Basis:* The First Amendment prohibits state establishment of religion and requires the separation of church and state. The Court finds the program allowing the use of state buildings for religious instruction and providing state support of religious class attendance, through application of the compulsory attendance law, to be unconstitutional because it fails to maintain the required separation of church and state.

## ZORACH v. CLAUSON, 343 U.S. 306 (1952)

*Facts:* New York City had a program of "released time" religious instruction under which public school students are permitted, on their parents' written request, to leave the building during school hours to go to religious centers for instruction or prayer. The students who are not released for religious purposes are required to stay in school. All costs of the program and all

18

facilities for it are paid for and provided by the religious organizations. Public funds are not expended for the program and religious classes are not held in the public school buildings. Taxpayers, who are residents of New York City and whose children attend its public schools, challenged the present law, contending it is in essence not different from the one involved in *McCollum (supra)*.

*Holding:* (6x3) A law that allows public schools to adjust their schedules in order to release children for religious instruction outside the schools' facilities and that requires no state financial support of such instruction is constitutional.

*Basis:* By releasing children from school for religious instruction, the state has not acted counter to the First Amendment which prohibits laws creating a state establishment of religion and laws denying the free exercise of religion.

## ENGEL v. VITALE, 370 U.S. 421 (1962)

*Facts:* A local board of education, acting under authority of a New York State law, ordered a 22-word nondenominational prayer to be said aloud by each class, in the presence of a teacher, at the beginning of each school day. The prayer had been composed by the Board of Regents which had also established the procedure for its recitation. Those children not wishing to pray were to be excused from the exercise.

Parents brought this action to challenge the constitutionality of both the state law which authorized the school district to mandate the use of prayer in public schools and the school district's action of ordering recitation of this particular prayer.

*Holding:* (5/1x1) State encouragement of the regular recitation of prayer in the public school system is unconstitutional.

*Basis:* The statute providing for prayer recitation in the public schools is in direct violation of the First Amendment prohibition of a state establishment of religion.

## ABINGTON SCHOOL DISTRICT v. SCHEMPP, MURRAY v. CURLETT, 374 U.S. 203 (1963)

*Facts:* A Pennsylvania law required that 10 Bible verses be read with no comment at the beginning of the school day. The Bible readings were to be followed by the recitation of the Lord's Prayer, held in the school building and conducted by public school personnel. On written parental request, a child could be excused from the exercise. Baltimore adopted a similar rule for its school system. The Schempp and Murray families challenged the constitutionality of the practice required by state statute and local regulations, respectively.

**Holding:**
(5/3x1) It is unconstitutional for a state law to promote the reading of verses from the Bible and the recitation of prayer on school grounds under the supervision of school personnel during school hours, even when attendance is not compulsory.

**Basis:**
The establishment clause of the First Amendment, made applicable to the states by the Fourteenth Amendment, requires the states to be neutral toward religion and forbids state establishment of religion. A law requiring a prayer at the beginning of the school day is an impermissible establishment of religion, whether or not students are forced to participate.

## CHAMBERLIN v. DADE COUNTY BOARD OF PUBLIC INSTRUCTION, 377 U.S. 402 (1964)

**Facts:**
A Florida statute required devotional Bible reading and the recitation of prayers in the Florida public schools. The state supreme court found the statute to be constitutional. The Florida decision was challenged in this action.

**Holding:**
(per curiam 6/3x0) A state statute may not authorize the reading of Bible verses and the recitation of prayer on school grounds, during school hours, and under the supervision of school personnel.

**Basis:**
This case follows *Abington School District v. Schempp (supra),* in which the Court held that school prayer laws are in violation of the First and Fourteenth Amendments in that they are a state establishment of religion.

## BOARD OF EDUCATION v. ALLEN, 392 U.S. 236 (1968)

**Facts:**
A New York State law required local public school authorities to lend textbooks free of charge to both public and private school students in grades seven through twelve. In this case, a

local school board, desiring to block the allocation of state funds for students of private, religious schools, challenged the constitutionality of the statute.

*Holding:* (5/1x3) A law which provides for the state-subsidized loan of secular textbooks to private, as well as to public, school students is constitutional.

*Basis:* The First Amendment proscribes laws which create a state establishment of religion. Since the books loaned are part of a general program to further the secular education of all students and are not, in fact, used to teach religion, the program is not therefore an establishment of religion. The Court also notes that the state aid goes to parents and students rather than to the religious schools directly and therefore would not be a state establishment of religion.

## WALZ v. TAX COMMISSION, 397 U.S. 664 (1970)

*Facts:* A New York City law provides property tax exemptions for nonprofit religious, educational, or charitable enterprises. A real estate owner argued that the exemption indirectly requires him to make a contribution to religious institutions and therefore is unconstitutional.

*Holding:* (6/2x1) A law permitting a tax exemption for nonprofit religious, educational, or charitable enterprises is constitutional.

*Basis:* The First Amendment prohibits the state establishment of religion and the excessive entanglement of the church and the state. Tax exemptions for religious institutions are historically sanctioned as being neutral toward, rather than supportive of, religion. The Court finds that such exemptions lessen, rather than increase, church-state entanglement.

## LEMON v. KURTZMAN, EARLEY v. DICENSO, 403 U.S. 602 (1971) ("Lemon I")

*Facts:* This case raised questions about Pennsylvania and Rhode Island statutes which provided for state aid to church-related elementary and secondary schools. Both statutes were enacted with the objective of aiding the quality of secular education in the nonpublic schools. The constitutionality of both statues was challenged.

21

The Rhode Island statute supplemented the salaries of teachers of secular subjects in nonpublic elementary schools so that these schools could attract competent teachers. The supplement could not exceed 15% of the teacher's annual salary, and the salary itself, when supplemented, could not exceed the maximum paid public school teachers. The teacher had to be certified, to be employed at a nonpublic school at which the average per-pupil expenditure on secular education was less than the average in the public schools, to teach only courses offered in the public schools, and to use only instructional materials used in the public schools. Teachers also had to agree in writing not to teach a course in religion. In Rhode Island the nonpublic elementary schools serve about 25% of the student population, and about 95% of these schools are affiliated with the Roman Catholic church.

The Pennsylvania statute authorized the state to reimburse nonpublic schools solely for their actual expenditures for teachers' salaries, textbooks, and instructional materials which were used for secular courses. The subsidized course had to be also offered by the public schools. The nonpublic schools had to maintain prescribed accounting procedures and had to have texts and instructional materials approved by the state. The statute benefited schools which served more than 20% of the total number of students in the state. More than 96% of these students attended church-related schools, most of which were affiliated with the Roman Catholic church.

*Holding:*    (5/3x1) (1) A law providing a state subsidy for nonpublic school teachers' salaries is unconstitutional, even where the funds are paid only to teachers of secular subjects. (2) A law providing for state reimbursement to nonpublic schools for expenses incurred in the teaching of secular subjects is also unconstitutional.

*Bases:*    Both statutes are unconstitutional under the establishment clause of the First Amendment insofar as they create an excessive entanglement between government and religion. To be valid, a statute must (1) have a secular legislative purpose; (2) have a principal effect which neither advances nor inhibits religion; and (3) not foster "an excessive government entanglement with religion." As to the Rhode Island program, state-subsidized teachers would have to be monitored extensively by the state to assure that they did not teach religion. This would involve an excessive entanglement between church and state. As to the Pennsylvania program, the aid would be directly given to the nonpublic schools. This combined with the surveillance and accounting procedures that would be required, would create excessive church-state entanglement and excessive state support of religion.

## JOHNSON v. SANDERS, 319 F. Supp. 421 (D. Conn. 1970), *aff'd,* 403 U.S. 955 (1971)

*Facts:*    A 1969 Connecticut act authorized the state to reimburse private schools for part of the expenses for texts and teachers' salaries incurred by them in the teaching of secular subjects. The act would require extensive state regulation of the religious schools which make up the majority of potential beneficiaries since it would require that state funds be used only for secular texts and secular teachers' salaries. In addition, the act would mandate that a fraction of the student body of each beneficiary school be admitted on a nonreligious basis. The fraction would equal the percentage of the total yearly budget of the school paid by state funds under the act. In this case, state residents and taxpayers challenged the constitutionality of this aid to sectarian schools.

*Decision:*    Summarily affirmed (8x1)

*Holding:*    (of the three-judge lower court) A state law reimbursing religious schools for the teaching of secular courses and resulting in state support of education in a setting surrounded by sectarian observances and offered to a student body largely restricted to a religious group is unconstitutional. Such a law requiring extensive state regulation of the daily operation of religious schools in order to assure that state funds are used to pay only for secular texts and teachers is unconstitutional.

*Bases:*    The establishment clause of the First Amendment prohibits laws which result in state sponsorship of, or excessive involvement with, religion. (1) The state support of secular courses taught in religious school surroundings and to a sectarian student body is unconstitutional state support of religion. (2) The state regulation of the sectarian schools in their use of the subsidy funds would result in excessive entanglement between church and state.

23

49433

## WISCONSIN v. YODER, 406 U.S. 205 (1972)

*Facts:* Members of the Old Order Amish religious community, a Christian sect that has been a distinct and identifiable group for three centuries, were convicted of violating Wisconsin's compulsory school attendance law. The law required parents to send their children to school until age sixteen. The Amish refused to send their children to any formal school, public or private, beyond the eighth grade because they believed that further formal education would seriously impede their children's preparation for adult life and for religious practice within the Amish communities. The Amish did provide their teenagers with substantial practical training at home for Amish adulthood. Further, it was shown that the children would most likely be self-sufficient citizens. The Amish challenged the constitutionality of the school attendance law as applied to them.

*Holding:* (5½/3x½) Where compulsory school attendance beyond the eighth grade will have a detrimental effect on an established religious community's way of life in which religious belief and practice are inseparable from daily work, the compulsory attendance law must yield to the parents' desires as to the form of their children's education.

*Basis:* The compulsory attendance law violates the free exercise clause of the First Amendment. Since the religious belief and practice of the Amish is inseparable from their daily way of life, a law that interferes with Amish life also infringes upon the free exercise of their religion. The state may infringe on this right only for a compelling reason. Since the Amish way of life is not analogous to a health or safety hazard to the children and does not tend to create adults incapable of responsible citizenship or self-sufficiency, the state cannot successfully argue that it is empowered as *parens patrie* to override the parents' interest for the benefit of their children.

## LEMON v. KURTZMAN, 411 U.S. 192 (1973) *("Lemon II")*

*Facts:* A Pennsylvania law had provided for state reimbursement of sectarian schools for secular education functions that they performed. The state was to monitor the programs to assure that state funds were spent on only secular courses of instruction. No attempts were made to enjoin the operation of

24

the program, although a law suit challenging the law's validity was begun soon after it was passed. Relying on the statute, sectarian schools entered into contracts with the state for performance of and compensation for services. The Court later invalidated the statute in *Lemon I (supra)*. The federal district court then enjoined the state for reimbursement for services performed after the law was invalidated but permitted payments for services performed prior to that date, including services performed during the 1970-71 school year. In this case, the propriety of state payments to religious schools for services performed in 1970-71 was challenged.

*Holding:*    (4/1x3) Religious schools that contract for reimbusement under a state law reasonably presumed to be valid and that are to be compensated for only secular services performed prior to judicial invalidation of the relevant state law may be allowed to receive the compensation for which they contracted.

*Bases:*    (1) The district court is permitted broad discretion in fashioning a remedy. Here, it reasonably permitted payment for services rendered in reliance on the law's validity. (2) There is no violation of the First Amendment establishment clause since no excessive entanglement between church and state can result because the program cannot continue beyond these final payments; and the services, that have already been performed by the religious schools, were monitored in order to assure that they were secular in nature.

## LEVITT v. COMMISSION FOR PUBLIC EDUCATION AND RELIGIOUS LIBERTY, 413 U.S. 472 (1973)

*Facts:*    A New York State statute enabled the legislature to appropriate funds to reimburse nonpublic schools for the performance of various services required by the state. Of these services, the most expensive is the administration, grading, compiling, and reporting of test results. There are two types of tests administered in the schools: the state-prepared tests, such as Regents exams and student aptitude tests; and the traditional in-school, teacher-prepared tests. The latter make up the overwhelming majority of the tests. A lump sum per pupil was allotted annually under the statute and the beneficiary nonpublic schools were not required to account for the money received or to specify how it was spent. In this case, a group of New York State taxpayers challenged the validity of the statute.

25

*Holding:*        (8x1) A statute which authorizes the state to reimburse nonpublic schools for state-required student services, e.g., testing, and which does not limit such reimbursement to the secular functions of such schools is unconstitutional.

*Basis:*        The First Amendment proscribes laws creating a state establishment of religion. Where the state allocates funds directly to religious schools, and especially where the use of such funds is not limited to secular functions, there is impermissible state support of religion.

## COMMITTEE FOR PUBLIC EDUCATION AND RELIGIOUS LIBERTY v. NYQUIST, 413 U.S. 756 (1973)

*Facts:*        The State of New York established three financial aid programs for nonpublic elementary and secondary schools. One program was to supply funds to qualifying nonpublic schools for repair and maintenance of equipment and facilities. Another provided for a tuition reimbursement to low-income parents with children enrolled in elementary or secondary nonpublic schools. The third program provided for a state income tax credit to middle-income parents with children enrolled in nonpublic schools. Most of the schools that were to benefit from these programs were sectarian schools. A group of taxpayers challenged the validity of the laws authorizing the expenditure of state funds for the benefit of such institutions.

*Holding:*        (6/1x2) (1) A law providing for direct payments to sectarian schools for repair and maintenance of equipment and facilities is unconstitutional, even when limited to 50% of comparable state aid to public schools. (2) Tuition reimbursements and income tax credits for parents of nonpublic school children are unconstitutional, even if the dollar amount of the reimbursements is a statistically small portion of the total tuitions paid.

*Bases:*        To meet the requirement of the establishment clause of the First Amendment, a state law must (1) reflect a clearly secular legislative purpose; (2) have a primary effect that neither advances nor inhibits religion; and (3) avoid excessive government entanglement with religion. In this case, the repair and maintenance provisions directly support the religious as well as the secular functions of the beneficiary schools and therefore unconstitutionally advance religion; the tax

26

provisions directly support the enrollment of children in religious schools and therefore unconstitutionally advance religion; and the potential for continuing political strife over further appropriations to aid religion creates an excessive state entanglement with religion.

## SLOAN v. LEMON, 413 U.S. 825 (1973)

*Facts:*    In an earlier case, *Lemon I (supra),* the Court ruled that a law aiding nonpublic elementary and secondary education was unconstitutional. The law in that case provided for reimbursement of sectarian schools for expenses incurred in the teaching of nonsectarian courses. The Court ruled that the state supervision necessary to guarantee that the aid would benefit only secular activities would foster "excessive entanglement" between church and state. In an attempt to avoid the entanglement problem, the Pennsylvania legislature enacted a law under which the state could reimburse parents with children in nonpublic schools for a portion of their tuition expenses. This new law specifically precluded state regulation of the schools and imposed no restrictions on the uses to which allotments could be put by beneficiary parents. In this case, the validity of the new law was challenged.

*Holding:*    (7x2) A law providing for state reimbursement of parents with children enrolled in sectarian schools for tuition paid to such schools is unconstitutional.

*Basis:*    The First Amendment proscribes laws creating a state establishment of religion. State payment to parents of children in sectarian schools encourages enrollment in such schools and therefore unconstitutionally supports religion with state funds.

## WHEELER v. BARRERA, 417 U.S. 402 (1974)

*Facts:*    Title I, which provides funding for remedial programs for educationally deprived children in areas with a high concentration of children from low-income families, is the first federal aid-to-education program authorizing assistance for private, as well as public, school children. The primary responsibility for designing and effectuating a Title I program rests with the "local educational agency," e.g., the local school board. The plan must then be approved by the state educational agency and by the U.S. Commissioner of Education. In order to be

27

approved at the state level the plan must provide eligible private school students with services that are "comparable in quality, scope, and opportunity for participation to those provided for public school children with needs of equally high priority." The law does not require that identical services be provided nor does it intend that state constitutional spending proscriptions, e.g., those against the use of public funds to employ private school teachers, be preempted as a condition for accepting federal funds.

Although most of Missouri's Title I money was spent to employ remedial teachers, state officials had refused to appropriate any money to pay nonpublic school teachers working during regular school hours. However, some Title I funds were allocated to nonpublic schools. In this case, parents of nonpublic school students argued that state school officials were illegally approving Title I programs that did not offer comparable services to their children.

*Holding:*    (5/3x1) Title I's requirement that comparable services be provided to private school children does not require a state to administer a program calling for the use of Title I teachers in nonpublic schools during regular school hours. Where such a program would be contrary to state law, officials may formulate alternative plans.

*Basis:*    The decision is based on Title I's requirement that comparable, although not identical, services be provided for eligible private school students. The issue of whether or not the First Amendment would permit Title I subsidy of teachers working within nonpublic schools is not decided in this case.

## MEEK v. PITTENGER, 421 U.S. 349 (1975)

*Facts:*    In order to assure that nonpublic school children would receive auxiliary services, textbooks, and instructional materials which were provided free to public school children, the Pennsylvania General Assembly passed two acts in 1972. Act 194 authorized state provision of auxiliary services including counseling, testing, and remedial education for the educationally disadvantaged. These services were to be provided within the nonpublic schools but staffed by employees of the public school system. Act 195 authorized the lending of secular textbooks, either directly or through an intermediary, to nonpublic school children. It also authorized the lending of other instructional

28

materials and equipment directly to the nonpublic schools. The great majority of schools that were to benefit from the laws were sectarian schools. In this case, the validity of the two acts was challenged.

*Holding:*   (3/3x3) (1) An act authorizing the state-subsidized loan of secular texts to nonpublic, as well as to public school students, is constitutional. (2) An act authorizing substantial direct aid to the educational function of sectarian schools is unconstitutional. State provisions of personnel or of instructional materials that could be used for religious, as well as secular, education constitutes such substantial direct aid and therefore is unconstitutional.

*Basis:*   The establishment clause of the First Amendment, made applicable to the states by the Fourteenth Amendment, prohibits state support of religious institutions. While the Court allows the state loan of secular texts to nonpublic, as well as to public, school children, it finds that the provision of millions of dollars of additional aid to sectarian schools is too direct and substantial an aid to the total educational function of such schools to be constitutional. The provision of staff or of materials, susceptible of use in religious, as well as secular, instruction is unconstitutional because it would require excessive state entanglement with religious institutions in order to insure that state aid is not used to support the religious function of such institutions. The Court also notes the probability of political entanglement as the result of legal suits over future appropriations of funds largely for the benefit of sectarian schools.

## ROEMER v. BOARD OF PUBLIC WORKS, 426 U.S. 736 (1976)*

*Facts:*   A Maryland statute authorized state aid to any private institution of higher learning within the state which met certain minimum criteria. Excluded were institutions which award only seminarian or theological degrees. The aid was in the form of an annual subsidy based on the number of students enrolled, but not including those enrolled in religious programs of study.

---

*For similar cases permitting state aid (construction funds for building to be used for secular purposes) to church-affiliated institutions of higher education see *Tilton v. Richardson*, 403 U.S. 672 (1971) and *Hunt v. McNair*, 413 U.S. 734 (1973). These cases include in their reasoning the distinction made in *Roemer* between higher education and elementary-secondary education in terms of the pervasiveness of the religious influence.

More than two-thirds of the colleges receiving aid had no religious affiliation. Institutions found eligible under the statute were required to use the funds only for secular purposes, to keep them in a separate account, and to keep records of their expenditure. These records were subject to review by a state agency to assure secular use of the funds. In this case, Maryland citizens and taxpayers challenged the program and statute as unconstitutional.

*Holding:*      (3/2x4) A state statute that provides financial aid to private institutions of higher education having student bodies not primarily enrolled in religiously-oriented programs, that requires such aid be spent only for secular purposes, and that establishes a system of reporting of accounts to insure that funds are so spent is constitutional.

*Bases:*      In order to be constitutional a statute must (1) have a secular legislative purpose; (2) have a primary effect which neither advances or inhibits religion; and (3) not result in excessive church-state entanglement. In addition to finding the statute to conform to the first part of this three-part test, the Court distinguished between education in kindergarten through eighth grade and higher education in applying parts two and three of the test. More specifically, the Court concludes that the religious element is less pervasive in church-related colleges and universities than in parochial elementary and secondary schools.

**WOLMAN v. WALTER, 45 U.S.L.W. 4861 (June 24, 1977)**

*Facts:*      A recent Ohio law providing state aid to nonpublic elementary and secondary schools was challenged by a group of citizens and taxpayers. Most of the schools standing to benefit from the program are sectarian institutions.

    The statute authorizes the provisions of the following: (1) secular texts, (2) standardized testing and diagnostic services, (3) therapeutic and remedial services administered by public school personnel at religiously neutral locations, (4) instructional materials and equipment comparable to those supplied to public schools, and (5) transportation and other services for field trips.

*Holding:*      (6½x2½) A state may constitutionally supply sectarian private schools with the following: (1) secular texts which are approved by public school authorities and which are loaned to private school students or their parents, (2) standardized tests and scorings services such as are used in the public schools, provided that nonpublic school personnel are not involved in test drafting or scoring and nonpublic schools are not reimbursed for costs of test administration, (3) diagnostic speech, hearing, and psychological services performed in the nonpublic schools by public school personnel, and (4) therapeutic guidance and remedial services staffed by public school personnel and performed in religiously neutral territory, i.e., not on private school grounds. A state may not constitutionally provide nonpublic schools with instructional equipment and materials or with field trip transportation and services.

*Bases:*    A statute, under the establishment clause of the First Amendment, must have a secular legislative purpose, a principal effect that is religiously neutral, and must not foster excessive government entanglement with religion. By this standard, the state provision of secular texts, standardized tests, diagnostic and therapeutic or remedial services as described above is constitutional. The loan of instructional materials to the private schools rather than to individual students is excessive state aid to the advancement of religion and is unconstitutional. The state support of nonpublic school field trips is a benefit to sectarian education rather than to individual students and is therefore unconstitutional state aid to sectarian education. Also, the state surveillance of field trips which would be required to insure their secular nature would result in unconstitutional church-state entanglement.

# III. STUDENT RIGHTS AND RESPONSIBILITIES

*Reviewers:* Henry S. Lufler, Jr.
Assistant Dean
School of Education
University of Wisconsin

Michael A. Roth
Student
School of Law
Harvard University

Traditionally, the U.S. Supreme Court has been reluctant to interfere in school matters related to the rights and responsibilities of students. A number of reasons explain this orientation, with perhaps the major one being the strong belief of the judiciary in the American tradition of local control over the schools. In *Epperson v. Arkansas* the Court stated that "Public education in our nation is committed to the control of state and local authorities. Courts do not and cannot intervene in the resolution of conflicts which arise in the daily operation of school systems." The first four cases in this chapter reflect the deference that the Court gave to local control in matters concerning student rights. In these cases the interests of local governments in protecting health, forbidding fraternities, and promoting good citizenship were upheld in the face of Fourteenth Amendment challenges by students.

In 1943, the Court issued two opinions in flag saluting cases which signaled a later change in judicial attitude toward the rights of students versus those of state and local governments. However, in upholding the First Amendment rights to belief and expression of students, it is not clear if the Court had changed its approach to student rights or whether these decisions were simply a by-product of the Court's emerging interest in protecting fundamental rights against government encroachment. The fact that the Court did not decide another student rights case until 26 years later seems to support the latter interpretation.

The Court in 1967, held that due process rights must be afforded to those under, as well as over, the age of eighteen. Although the *Gault* decision was not a school case, this decision, which is discussed in this chapter, seemed to trigger a renewed interest by the Court in the rights and responsibilities of students. The Court then proceeded to hand down nine decisions in this area in the next ten years.

The *Tinker* case in 1969, marked the Court's first foray into the student rights field since its decision in *Barnette*. Again the issue was the First Amendment rights to belief and expression of students, and again the Court upheld the status of students as "persons" under the Constitution. This time the interest of students in expressing themselves by wearing black arm bands was deemed to outweigh the fear of disturbance on the part of school authorities. The next four cases: *Mosley, Grayned, Healy,* and *Papish,* all followed the course set by the Court in *Tinker* by upholding various First Amendment rights of students, including the right to picket, the right of association, and freedom of speech and of the press.

From 1967-1974, all of the school cases decided by the Supreme Court involved various substantive interests of students. In 1975, the Court in the *Goss* case expanded the procedural rights of students faced with short-term suspensions by requiring notice and an opportunity to be heard prior to suspension. The Court further strengthened the procedural rights of students in *Wood v. Strickland,* which followed shortly after *Goss.* In *Wood* the Court held that a school official is not immune from liability for money damages in cases where the constitutional rights of the student are abrogated. Finally, in that same year, the Court summarily affirmed a holding of a three-judge federal district court in *Baker v. Owen* that corporal punishment is constitutional if students are afforded certain procedural safeguards prior to its administration.

The decisions of the Court in *Goss, Wood,* and *Baker* that provided for and strengthened the procedural rights of students under the due process clause of the Fourteenth Amendment are perhaps best viewed, along with *Gault,* as part of a general expansion by the Court of procedural safeguards to various private liberty and property interests, and not as part of a new judicial attitude toward the schools. The Court's holding in the 1977 *Ingraham* case seems to support this interpretation. In this case the Court again upheld the constitutionality of corporal punishment in schools, but refused to require any notice or hearing prior to its implementation. This case, when taken with other contemporary non-school cases, seems to represent a reluctance on the part of the present Court to extend further due process requirements into new areas. It should be noted at the same time that it does not appear the Court will discontinue its protection of the substantive constitutional rights of students.

## JACOBSON v. MASSACHUSETTS, 197 U.S. 11 (1905)

*Facts:*     State law empowered the board of health of a city or town to require the vaccination of all its inhabitants and to provide free vaccinations if such action was necessary for the public health or safety. Children who should not be vaccinated for medical reasons were excused from compliance with the order. Noting

33

an increase in the incidence of smallpox within the city, Cambridge health officials instituted a program of mandatory vaccination. In this case, an adult resident of Cambridge sought to have the program declared unconstitutional.

*Holding:*    (7x2) A law that mandates compulsory vaccination in order to protect the public health and that does not require that one whose health does not permit vaccination to participate in the program is constitutional.

*Basis:*    The Fourteenth Amendment protects persons from arbitrary state action infringing on life, liberty, or property interests. However, state laws which infringe on personal liberty but are reasonable measures taken by the legislature to protect the public health and safety are constitutional. The states have a "police power" to protect the public health, safety, and welfare.

## WAUGH v. BOARD OF TRUSTEES, 237 U.S. 589 (1915)

*Facts:*    A state law prohibited Greek letter fraternities in the state's higher educational facilities and denied students who joined such organizations the opportunity to work toward honors or diplomas. Students who were already members of such organizations at the time of the law's passage would suffer no penalty under the act if they became inactive members. A student challenged the constitutionality of the statute.

*Holding:*    (9x0) A law penalizing membership in university Greek letter fraternities by denying active or new members of such groups access to the state's higher educational facilities is constitutional.

*Basis:*    The Fourteenth Amendment prohibits state action which impairs a person's liberty, life, or property interest without due process of law or which denies a person equal protection of the law. Viewing access to the state's colleges and universities as a privilege rather than a right, the Court finds that no property interest under the Fourteenth Amendment is impaired by the statute. Nor does the Court find a denial of equal protection in the law's distinction between those already members of fraternities and prospective members. It finds that the allowance made for those already members is reasonable and prevents unfair penalization for conduct that was not forbidden until the statute took effect.

## ZUCHT v. KING, 260 U.S. 174 (1922)

*Facts:*        Ordinances of the city of San Antonio, Texas, provided that no child or other person shall attend a public school or other place of education without first having presented a certificate of vaccination. In accord with this law, public officials excluded a student from both public and private schools because she was not vaccinated and refused to be vaccinated. The student argued that there was, at the time, no medical situation requiring vaccination and that the law is overboard in that (1) it makes vaccination mandatory; and (2) it leaves enforcement to the board of health without limiting the board's discretion.

*Holding:*      (9x0) A vaccination law conditioning public and private school attendance on compulsory vaccination and leaving the operation of the vaccination program to the board of health is constitutional.

*Basis:*        The police power of the states enables them to mandate compulsory vaccination in order to safeguard the public health, safety, and welfare. The fact that the board of health is given broad discretion in the implementation of the program does not invalidate the statute.

## MINERSVILLE SCHOOL DISTRICT v. GOBITIS, 310 U.S. 586 (1940)*

*Facts:*        The local school board required all public school students and teachers to salute the American flag as part of a daily school exercise. Two children who refused to salute the flag because of religious convictions were denied education in the public schools. They challenged the validity of the compulsory flag salute regulations.

*Holding:*      (7/1x1) A school board regulation requiring students and teachers to salute the American flag, even if to do so is contrary to their religious belief, is constitutional. Avenues for criticism and change of the regulation must be left open. The school board may not suppress the expression of opposing views made privately between parents and children or publicly in order to urge modification of the flag salute policy.

*Bases:*        The First Amendment guarantees of personal freedom of speech and belief are balanced against the right of the state to legislate measures reasonably likely to promote the survival of

*Reversed by *West Virginia State Board of Education.* v. *Barnette infra.*

the government and good citizenship. The flag salute ceremony is reasonably likely to support these goals and it is reasonable for the legislature to conclude that excusing some children from the exercise would diminish its unifying, patriotic effect. In addition, the impairment of First Amendment freedoms is ameliorated by the retention of the personal right to work in an orderly and legal way for a change in the policy and to teach one's children at home or in religious school the premises and priorities of one's religious belief. For these reasons, the mandatory flag salute law is constitutional.

## TAYLOR v. MISSISSIPPI, 319 U.S. 583 (1943)

*Facts:*   Under a state statute, teaching or encouraging others not to "salute, honor or respect . . ." the national or state flags was a criminal offense. Several members of the Jehovah's Witnesses, who were convicted for expressing their religious belief that flag saluting and nationalism are unchristian, challenged the constitutionality of the statute. The literature that they distributed specifically criticized the practice of opening flag salute exercises in public schools.

*Holding:*   (9x0) The state may not punish those who, for religious reasons, urge and advise that people cease saluting the national and state flags.

*Basis:*   The First Amendment, which is made applicable to the states by the Fourteenth Amendment, protects the rights of freedom of expression and of belief from arbitrary governmental intrusion. Unless accompanied by subversive intent or the creation of a clear and present danger to the government, the expression of opinion cannot constitutionally be burdened with criminal sanctions.

## WEST VIRGINIA STATE BOARD OF EDUCATION v. BARNETTE, 319 U.S. 624 (1943)

*Facts:*   Public school pupils were expelled for their failure to participate in a compulsory flag salute program. As a result, students became liable to prosecution as delinquents and their parents became liable for noncompliance with the compulsory education law. The students challenged the constitutionality of the school board's action of conditioning public school attendance on compliance with a mandatory flag salute program.

36

*Holding:*        (3/3x3) Public school officials may not require students to salute and pledge allegiance to the flag at the risk of punishment and expulsion from school. *Gobitis (supra)* is thus explicitly overruled.

*Basis:*        The First Amendment protects expressions of political opinion and symbolic speech. The refusal to salute the flag is an expression of opinion within the meaning of this Amendment. The Fourteenth Amendment prohibits state impairment of First Amendment rights absent a present and substantial danger to interests which the state may lawfully protect. The mere passive refusal to salute the flag does not create a danger to the state such that the First Amendment rights to belief and expression may be impaired.

## *In re* GAULT, 387 U.S. 1 (1967)

*Facts:*        A 15-year-old boy was taken into custody as the result of a complaint that he had made an obscene phone call. After several hearings at which the boy was not allowed to confront the complaining witness and was not represented by legal counsel, the juvenile court sentenced him to a maximum of six years in a state school for juvenile delinquents. If an adult were to have been found guilty of the same act, the maximum penalty would have been two months imprisonment and a $50 fine. There was no provision for appeal of juvenile court decisions to a higher court. In this case, the boy's parents challenged the validity of the state juvenile court statute which allows a child to be incarcerated yet denies him basic constitutional rights.

*Holding:*        (5/2½x1½) When juvenile court proceedings could result in a minor's incarceration in an institution, the following constitutional safeguards must be provided: (1) timely and adequate written notice of the charges must be given to the minor and his/her parents or guardian; (2) parents or guardians and the child must be informed of their right to legal counsel, and, if they are unable to afford a lawyer, counsel will be appointed by the court to represent them; (3) the constitutional privilege against self-incrimination is applicable to these proceedings; and (4) absent a valid confession, a child has a right to cross-examine hostile witnesses and to present his/her own witnesses.

*Basis:*        The Fifth Amendment creates a right against self-incrimination in criminal matters. The Fourteenth Amendment protects the people from state action impairing life, liberty or property interests without due process of law. These amendments apply to those under, as well as over, the age of 18. Children faced with a loss of liberty must be afforded the procedural safeguards required by the due process clause of the Fourteenth Amendment.

## TINKER v. DES MOINES INDEPENDENT COMMUNITY SCHOOL DISTRICT, 393 U.S. 503 (1969)

*Facts:*     Three public school pupils who wore black arm bands to class in order to protest the government's policy in Vietnam were suspended from school. It was not shown that substantial interference with school work or school discipline had resulted or could reasonably have been predicted to result from the students' conduct. Based on a showing that school authorities did not prohibit the wearing of other symbols with political or controversial significance, the Court noted that the officials were interested in suppressing students' expressions of opinion about a specific subject, the Vietnam war. The students sought a court order restraining the officials from disciplining them and declaring the suspensions unconstitutional.

*Holding:*     (5/2x2) It is unconstitutional to suspend students for the peaceful wearing of arm bands or for other symbolic expression of opinion unless it can be shown that material interference with, or substantial disruption of, the school's routine did or would occur.

*Basis:*     The peaceful wearing of the arm bands is an expression of opinion entitled to protection under the First Amendment, which is made applicable to the states by the Fourteenth Amendment. Since students are "persons" under the Constitution, school officials may constitutionally infringe on students' First Amendment rights only when the particular expression of opinion proscribed would materially and substantially interfere with the operation of the school and the rights of other students to learn. Mere apprehension of disturbance is not a sufficient basis for such action on the part of school authorities.

## POLICE DEPARTMENT v. MOSLEY, 408 U.S. 92 (1972)

*Facts:*     A lone, peaceful picketer habitually demonstrated at a high school against alleged racial discrimination at the school. An

38

ordinance which was about to become effective provided as follows:

> A person commits disorderly conduct when he knowingly: (i) pickets or demonstrates on a public way within 150 feet of any primary or secondary school building while the school is in session and one-half hour before the the school is in session and one-half hour after the school session has been concluded, *provided that this subsection does not prohibit the peaceful picketing of any school involved in a labor dispute.* (emphasis added)

Since the picketer's demonstration was not related to a labor dispute, his conduct would be prohibited by the ordinance. In this case, the picketer sought to have the ordinance declared unconstitutional and to enjoin the police department from enforcing it.

*Holding:*   (7/1x2) An ordinance prohibiting all non-labor picketing near the schools while they are in session is unconstitutionally overbroad.

*Basis:*   Since picketing involves expressive conduct within the protection of the First Amendment, limitations on picketing are carefully scrutinized by the Court. They must be narrowly tailored to serve as a substantial, legitimate, governmental interest to be valid under the Fourteenth Amendment. Disruption must be imminent to validate an official ban on picketing, and the judgment as to the likelihood of disorder must be made on an individualized basis and not by means of broad classifications, especially not by means of classifications based on subject matter. Thus, the Court concluded that this discrimination violated the equal protection requirement of the Fourteenth Amendment.

## GRAYNED v. CITY OF ROCKFORD, 408 U.S. 104 (1972)

*Facts:*   A student was arrested for his part in a demonstration in front of an Illinois high school. He was tried and convicted of violating two city ordinances. He challenged their constitutionality, claiming that they were invalid on their face. The statutes in question are as follows:

> 1.   Anti-picketing ordinance:
>    A person commits disorderly conduct when he knowingly: (i) pickets or demonstrates on a public way within 150 feet of any primary or secondary school building while the school is in session and

one-half hour before the school is in session and one-half hour after the school session has been concluded, *provided that this subsection does not prohibit the peaceful picketing of any school involved in a labor dispute* . . . (emphasis added)

2. Anti-noise ordinance:
   [N]o person, while on the public or private grounds adjacent to any building in which a school or any class thereof is in session, shall willfully make or assist in the making of any noise or diversion which disturbs or tends to disturb the peace or good order of such school session or class thereof . . .

The anti-picketing ordinance in question is identical to a Chicago ordinance which the Supreme Court considered in *Police Department v. Mosley (supra)*. In that case a lone, peaceful picketer had been demonstrating in a place and at a time which the statute would prohibit, since his demonstration was not related to a labor dispute but was concerned with racial discrimination at the school he was picketing.

*Holding:*   (8/½x½) (1) An ordinance prohibiting all non-labor picketing near the schools while they are in session is unconstitutionally overbroad. (2) An ordinance prohibiting the willful making of noise incompatible with normal school activity and limited as to time (when school is in session) and place (adjacent to the school) is constitutional.

*Bases:*   (1) Since picketing involves expressive conduct within the protection of the First Amendment, limitations on picketing are carefully scrutinized by the Court. They must be narrowly tailored to serve a substantial legitimate governmental interest to be valid under the Fourteenth Amendment. Substantial disruption must be imminent to validate an official ban on picketing, and the judgment as to the likelihood of disorder must be made on an individualized basis and not by means of broad classifications, especially not by means of classifications based on subject matter. This same ordinance was invalidated in *Police Department v. Mosley (supra)*. (2) The anti-noise ordinance is not so vague as to be an unconstitutional denial of due process under the Fourteenth Amendment. It is properly limited as to time, place, and scope. It does not prohibit conduct protected by the First and Fourteenth Amendments since it punishes only conduct which actually disrupts or is about to disrupt normal school activities. Under the ordinance, the decision is to be made, as is proper, on an individualized basis.

# HEALY v. JAMES, 408 U.S. 169 (1972)

*Facts:*      State college students, who wished to form a local chapter of Students for a Democratic Society (SDS), applied for and were denied recognition as a campus organization, despite having met all the necessary requirements. The students asserted that their organization would function independently of the national SDS. The college president denied them recognition because he was not satisfied that the group was independent of the national SDS, an organization which he found to have a philosophy of disruption and violence in conflict with the college's declaration of student rights. Based on this assumed link with the national organization, he found that the group would be a "disruptive influence." Recognition would have entitled the group to use campus buildings for meetings and to communicate with students and teachers through the student newspaper and the school's bulletin boards. Its ability to function on campus was impaired by the denial of these facilities. The group challenged the constitutionality of the college's denial of recognition.

*Holding:*      (8/1x0) A state college may not deny the benefits of official recognition to a group unless the college can justify such nonrecognition. The basis for such justification cannot consist of an assumed link with some other organization (guilt by association), or of mere disagreement with the group's philosophy, or of the fear of disruption, unsupported by any evidence that the particular group is likely to disrupt the discipline or educational program of the school. A proper basis for nonrecognition would be evidence that the group refused to affirm its intention to abide by reasonable campus regulations, provided that such affirmance is an established prerequisite for recognition of any group.

*Basis:*      The First Amendment right of association is protected from state encroachment by the Fourteenth Amendment. The state may not impair First Amendment rights without a compelling reason to do so. In the school context, impairment is justified when the conduct proscribed "materially and substantially disrupt(s) the work and discipline of the school." Mere apprehension is insufficient. By refusing to grant recognition and the rights that accompany it to the group, the state college impaired the group's exercise of its right of association.

41

# PAPISH v. BOARD OF CURATORS, 410 U.S. 667 (1973)

*Facts:*  A graduate student was expelled from a state university because she distributed on campus a newspaper containing an "indecent" cartoon. The cartoon depicted policemen raping the Statue of Liberty and the Goddess of Justice. The caption under the cartoon read: " . . . With Liberty and Justice for All." The student challenged the constitutionality of her dismissal.

*Holding:*  (6x3) The mere dissemination of ideas via a student publication, no matter how offensive to good taste, may not be barred from a university campus in the name of "conventions of decency." Unless it causes actual or imminent disruption of the university, or is legally obscene, a publication cannot constitutionally be suppressed, although reasonable regulation as to the time, manner, and place of distribution may be permissible.

*Basis:*  The First Amendment, as applied to the state through the Fourteenth Amendment, protects freedom of speech and of the press on the state college campus. Unless the newspaper is obscene, it is a constitutionally protected publication. Its content cannot be suppressed by state action on the campus in the absence of actual or imminent disruption of the discipline or educational process of the school.

# GOSS v. LOPEZ, 419 U.S. 565 (1975)

*Facts:*  The Ohio public school law empowered the principal to suspend students for up to ten days without giving them notice of the reasons for such action or hearing which would afford them an opportunity to explain their view of the incident in question. Nine high school students, who were suspended for ten days without a hearing of any kind, challenged the constitutionality of the statutes involved. They sought court orders restraining the school officials from issuing future suspensions and requiring the school officials to remove references to the past suspensions from their school records.

*Holding:*  (5x4) Suspensions ordered and statutes permitting students to be suspended without notice and hearing are unconstitutional. Students who are suspended for up to ten days must be accorded the following before a suspension: (1) oral or written notice of the charges; (2) an explanation of the evidence if the student denies the charges; and (3) some kind of hearing that includes an opportunity to present the student's view of the incident. There need be no delay in time between the notice and the subsequent hearing, and the constitutional requirements may be met by an informal discussion which includes the necessary elements. Unless a student's continued presence in the school poses a threat to persons, property, or the academic program, the required procedures shall precede suspension. If it is necessary that the student be removed immediately, the notice and hearing must follow within a reasonable time. Complicated fact situations and suspensions for longer periods of time may require more formal procedures which could include legal counsel and the right to present and confront witnesses.

*Bases:* The procedures applicable to short-term suspensions are required by the Fourteenth Amendment which prohibits the states from impairing a person's life, liberty, or property interest without due process of law. (1) The students have a "property" interest in public education. Although there is no constitutional provision guaranteeing free public education, the fact that the state has undertaken to provide its children with such an education creates a constitutionally protected interest. The state cannot deny compulsory education to some because of misconduct without adherence to the minimum procedures required by due process. (2) The students have a "liberty" interest in their reputations. Due process is required "where a person's good name is at stake . . . because of what the government is doing to him." The court finds that suspension could damage a student's reputation with teachers and other students and interfere with future educational and employment opportunities. Even if the damage to students' educational and reputational interest is temporary and slight, due process protections will still be required. The temporary nature of the impairment will determine "what process is due," but will not obviate the need for some procedural protection unless the impairment of rights is negligible.

## WOOD v. STRICKLAND, 420 U.S. 308 (1975)

*Facts:* Three high school students were expelled for violating school regulations because they put malt liquor in the punch served at an extracurricular meeting held at the school. The students and their parents brought suit under 42 U.S.C. section 1983, a federal statute which provides that any person who, under the color of state law, deprives anyone within the jurisdiction of the United States of constitutional rights or of rights secured by federal law, shall be liable to the party injured in a law suit for money damages or for other relief. The students sought money damages from two school administrators and from the members of the school board.

**Holding:**  (5/2x2) In the context of school discipline, a school official's immunity from liability for money damages sought under section 1983 depends on two elements of good faith: (1) The subjective element requires that to retain his/her immunity, the official acted in the sincere belief that he/she is doing right and without a "malicious intention to cause a deprivation of constitutional rights or other injury to the student." (2) The objective element causes the school official to lose his/her immunity if "[s]he knew or reasonably should have known that the action [s] he took . . . would violate the constitutional rights of the student affected . . . "

The objective part of the good faith requirement is satisfied if the official acts in accordance with the "students' clearly established constitutional rights" and with "settled, indisputable law."

**Basis:**  The Court finds that public policy and prior legal decisions require a qualified good faith immunity from damages for officials so that those who act in good faith and within the scope of their duties will not be intimidated in meeting their responsibilities by a fear of being sued.

In light of the importance of civil rights, the Court finds the objective element requiring the administrator to act in accord with the settled law and with the constitutional rights of those affected by official action to be a reasonable condition for their immunity from a law suit for damages. On the other hand, if a school official acts out of ignorance or in disregard to settled law, he or she may be sued.

Declining to consider questions of interpretation and application of the relevant school regulation, the Court notes that 42 U.S.C. section 1983 provides for federal court correction of only those improper exercises of discretion which result in violation of specific constitutional guarantees. The Court defers decision as to whether there had been a denial of procedural due process required by the Fourteenth Amendment, sending the case back to the lower court for initial consideration of that issue.

# BAKER v. OWEN, 395 F. Supp 294 (M.D.N.C.), *aff'd*, 423 U.S. 907 (1975)

*Facts:*     A North Carolina statute empowers school officials to "use reasonable force in the exercise of lawful authority to restrain or correct pupils and to maintain order." Although a mother had previously informed her son's teachers and principal that she did not want her son to be corporally punished because she disapproved of the practice, the boy was struck twice on the buttocks with a piece of wood because he disobeyed a rule forbidding the throwing of balls except during recess periods. In this case, the boy and his mother challenged the constitutionality of the statute and of the punishment inflicted under it.

*Decision:*   Summarily affirmed (9x0)

*Holding:*    (of the three-judge lower court) A statute allowing reasonable corporal punishment (punishment which causes no lasting discomfort or disability) for the purpose of maintaining order in the schools is constitutional if it is administered in accordance with the following procedural protections: (1) Except for acts of misconduct which are so anti-social or disruptive as to shock the conscience, corporal punishment may not be used unless the student has first been warned that the conduct for which he is being punished will occasion its use and unless other means have first been used to modify the student's behavior. (2) A second teacher or other school official must be present at the time the punishment is inflicted and must be informed, prior to its infliction and in the student's presence, of the reason for punishment. This affords the student an informal opportunity to raise his objection to arbitrary punishment. (3) The school official who adminstered the punishment must provide, on parental request, a written explanation of his/her reasons for punishment and the name of the second official who was present.

*Bases:*      (1) Although parents have a Fourteenth Amendment liberty interest in the control of the rearing and education of their children, that right does not preclude the state's use of reasonable punishment in order to achieve the legitimate goal of order in the schools. (2) The child's Fourteenth Amendment liberty interest in freedom from arbitrary infliction of even minimal corporal punishment mandates that some procedural safeguards be afforded to him/her.

45

# INGRAHAM v. WRIGHT, 97 S. Ct. 1401 (1977)

*Facts:*   Florida statute permits limited corporal punishment but requires prior consultation between the punishing teacher and the school principal and specifies that the punishment not be "degrading or unduly severe." In this case, punishment consisted of paddling two students with a flat wooden paddle. Lower court evidence suggested that the paddling was exceptionally harsh; one student required medical attention and missed eleven days of school, while the other reported loss of the full use of an arm for a week. The students argued that the severe paddling they received constituted cruel and unusual punishment in violation of the Eighth Amendment and deprived them of a liberty interest without a hearing as required by the Fourteenth Amendment.

*Holding:*   (5x4) Protection against excessive corporal punishment of students is provided by the opportunity to file civil or criminal complaints against school personnel. Therefore, neither a hearing is required before corporal punishment is administered nor is such punishment "cruel and unusual."

*Bases:*   (1) The cruel and unusual punishment clause of the Eighth Amendment does not apply to questions of discipline in public schools but is limited to protecting those convicted of a crime. (2) The due process clause of the Fourteenth Amendment does not require notice and hearing prior to imposition of corporal punishment. While corporal punishment in the public schools does involve a student's liberty interest, the Court holds that traditional common law remedies were sufficient to afford due process

The threat of civil suit and possible criminal action against school officials is sufficient to protect the student's due process rights in corporal punishment cases.

# IV.  EMPLOYEE RIGHTS AND RESPONSIBILITIES

*Reviewer:* Bernard Shulman
Superintendent of Schools
Canton, Massachusetts

This section presents issues under the general topic of employee rights and responsibilities. Such issues have been and will continue to be addressed by the U.S. Supreme Court. Reference must be made not only to local state statutes dealing with employee relations, but also to the federal laws and the U.S. Constitution itself. As the cases in this chapter will indicate, an employee right may be founded in a local ordinance, a state statute, the federal Civil Rights Act, in one of the Amendments to the U.S. Constitution, or in an employer-employee contractual agreement.

Whether the rights of a teacher will be held to be constitutionally protected will depend in part on the weight given the teacher's expressed right, as against the reasonableness of state action needed to operate and manage the schools efficiently and effectively. Attempts by the state to prohibit such teachings as foreign language in the *Meyer* case have been viewed by the Court as a deprivation of the teacher's right to practice the profession of teaching. Where recognized subject matter was prohibited because of a religious belief as in the *Epperson* theory of evolution case, the Court viewed the prohibition as contrary to the First Amendment.

The interpretation of tenure laws has become an area of chief concern in employee relationships for the Court during recent years. Since 1970, litigation in the area of tenure and employment contracts, e.g., *Sinderman* and *Roth,* has increased noticeably. The creation of a tenure right, its definition and validity, the issues affecting enforceability, and the remedies for breach of tenure contract involve both substantive and procedural due process.

Loyalty oaths have also been the subject of extensive review by the Court, and as the cases indicate, the nature and wording of the required oath is subject to careful scrutiny by the Court. The Court, as demonstrated in the opinions in this chapter, has formulated a doctrine that will strike down as unconstitutional for vagueness any loyalty oath which is unclear and/or

47

difficult for an employee to determine what conduct is covered by the law and what may be regarded as violative of the Fourteenth Amendment.

Reasonable residency requirements have been upheld recently on the rational basis test under the Fourteenth Amendment, and the courts have treated retirement laws as expectancies rather than rights. Protection has been given to a teacher's exercise of his/her right to participate in union activity for purposes of collective bargaining, and further protection has been given to a teacher's exercise of his/her right to speak on issues of public importance.

The cases noted in this section can assist in providing a framework for administrative reference. As the body of federal, state, and local enactment that deals with employer-employee relations continues to grow, guidelines must be formulated within the context and parameters of the U.S. Supreme Court decisions. The Court will continue to wrestle with the balance between the employee's individual right and the interest of the educational establishment as represented through the state. These cases also reveal that the shifting nature of the burden of proof is a controlling issue in understanding the opinions of the U.S. Supreme Court in the application of the First and Fourteenth Amendments.

## MEYER v. NEBRASKA, 262 U.S. 390 (1923)

*Facts:*     A state law prohibited the in-school teaching of any subject in a foreign language or of any modern foreign language to children who had not yet completed the eighth grade. The law extended to both public and private school teachers. A private school teacher was convicted for teaching German to a child who had not yet completed the eighth grade. He challenged the constitutionality of the law.

*Holding:*     (7/2x0) A state law which prohibits the teaching of modern foreign languages to children in kindergarten through eighth grade is unconstitutional.

*Basis:*     The Fourteenth Amendment protects individuals from arbitrary or unreasonable state action impairing life, liberty, or property interests. The right to practice the profession of teacher is a right protected by the Fourteenth Amendment. The stated purpose of the restriction on the right to teach is that children who know only English through grade eight will be better citizens. However, because there is no clear danger to the state that stems from younger children studying foreign languages, the reason given is unconstitutionally unreasonable and arbitrary. It is therefore insufficient to support the limitation on the right to teach.

48

# BARTELS v. IOWA, 262 U.S. 404 (1923)

*Facts:*  This case consolidated the appeals of parochial school teachers in Iowa and Ohio who were convicted of the violation of state statutes prohibiting the teaching of foreign languages to students who had not yet completed the eighth grade. The case also considered a request to enjoin enforcement of a Nebraska statute penalizing the teaching of foreign languages to young children in schools.

*Holding:*  (7x2) A state law forbidding, under penalty, the teaching in any private, parochial, or public school of any modern foreign language to any child who has not passed the eighth grade is unconstitutional.

*Bases:*  (1) The laws limiting the teaching of modern foreign languages improperly invade the Fourteenth Amendment liberty interests of teachers, parents, and students. (2) This decision is based on *Meyer v. Nebraska (supra.)*

# PHELPS v. BOARD OF EDUCATION, 300 U.S. 319 (1937)

*Facts:*  A New Jersey law provided that teachers who had served for at least three years could not be dismissed or be subjected to a salary reduction except for cause and after a hearing on the merits of the case. In 1933, the law was amended enabling local boards to reduce the salaries of such tenured teachers. The new law prohibited discrimination in payment between individuals in the same class of service and set a minimum beyond which boards could not go in reduction of salary. Pursuant to this law, a school board set up classifications and lowered salaries by varying percentages according to classification. Those in the higher pay brackets suffered a larger percentage reduction in pay than those in lower brackets. Consequently the lowest paid individuals in the higher pay brackets received less pay than the highest paid individuals in the lower bracket. In this case, teachers challenged the validity of school board action taken pursuant to the New Jersey law.

*Holding:*  (9x0) It is constitutional for a state tenure law to be amended to permit reduction of teacher salaries and for school boards to take action under such an amendment as long as they do not discriminate unfairly against individuals in any classification of school employees.

49

*Bases:* (1) Article I, section 10, of the U.S. Constitution prohibits laws which impair contract rights. However, the Court views the tenure laws as a statement of legislative policy, and thus subject to modification, rather than as a contract. (2) The Fourteenth Amendment prohibits state action denying persons the equal protection of the laws. However, the Court takes as reasonable the division of personnel into classes for the application of a percentage reduction in pay. The Court, noting that all individuals in a given class are treated alike, finds that the incidental inequalities resulting from the plan's operation are not sufficient to invalidate the plan under the Fourteenth Amendment.

## DODGE v. BOARD OF EDUCATION, 302 U.S. 74 (1937)

*Facts:* A state statute provided a $1500 annual annuity to teachers who reached the compulsory retirement age and an annual annuity ranging from $1000 to $1500 to teachers who took a voluntary early retirement after twenty-five years of service. In 1935, the statute was amended to reduce the annuity of all presently and prospectively retired teachers. In this case, teachers challenged the right of the state to reduce the annuities.

*Holding:* (9x0) A statute fixing terms of retirement and the amount of the annual annuity to be paid to teachers does not create a right to continuation of its terms for either presently or prospectively retired teachers and may be altered by further legislation.

*Basis:* Article I, section 10, of the U.S. Constitution forbids laws impairing contracts, and the due process clause of the Fourteenth Amendment prohibits state impairment of an individual's vested rights without due process of law. The Court finds that the statute providing for annuities was not a contract with the teachers but a policy of the state which the state could modify by further legislation. Since the payments were gratuities involving no agreement of the parties, then no vested rights accrued.

## INDIANA *ex rel.* ANDERSON v. BRAND, 303 U.S. 95 (1938)

*Facts:* A 1899 state law required that all contracts between teachers and school corporations be written, signed by the parties, and made a matter of public record. Each such contract was to specify the starting date, duration of employment, and the salary to be paid. The Teacher Tenure Act subsequently created in 1927 provided that teachers who had served for five or more successive years would have tenure and could be dismissed only for cause. In 1933, the Tenure Act was amended to exclude teachers in township schools from its coverage. A teacher in a township school challenged her loss of tenure caused by the 1933 amendment of the Tenure Act.

*Holding:*   (7x1) A teacher tenure act creates in teachers, qualifying under its terms, contractual rights which cannot be altered by the state without good reason. The state's modification of those terms as to township teachers is improper.

*Basis:*   Article I, section 10, of the Constitution prohibits laws impairing contract rights. The Court views the Teacher Tenure Act as a law creating contract rights in teachers. The state can modify, as an exercise of its police power, only if such modification is for the public good. The Teacher Tenure Act is reasonable in that it protects teachers from arbitrary school board action. Because the amendment to exclude township teachers is not beneficial to the public, it is not a valid exercise of the police power.

## GARNER v. BOARD of PUBLIC WORKS, 341 U. S. 716 (1951)

*Facts:*   A 1941 amendment to the Los Angeles city charter enabled the city to deny public employment to anybody who within the five years prior to the effective date of the amendment had advised, advocated, or taught the overthrow of the government by force or who belonged to organizations which so advocated. An ordinance passed in 1948 required that city employees swear that for the preceding five years they have not advocated or taught and do not and will not advocate or teach violent revolution, and neither have belonged to nor presently belong to such an organization. Employees who refused to take the oath were discharged. Here they challenged the constitutionality of the ordinance.

*Holding:*   (4/1½x3½) It is constitutional for an ordinance to require that city employees swear they have not been, are not, and will not be advocates of violent overthrow of the government or members of organizations which so advocate. It is assumed that the penalty of discharge from employment is utilized only when membership in such an organization is knowing rather than

51

innocent. Since the oath was held to be constitutional, all who refused to take it and were discharged should be given the opportunity to take the oath and resume employment.

**Bases:** (1) A law is unconstitutional if it is *ex post facto,* that is, if it punishes conduct which was lawful at the time it was done. The Court finds that since the 1941 amendment to the city charter barred from employment those who committed the acts proscribed by the 1948 oath, the oath could not successfully be challenged as *ex post facto.* (2) Bills of attainder are laws which act to punish a certain group without the benefit of a judicial trial. The Court finds no punishment involved in this case. Rather, the Court finds that the city's standards are reasonable and that its inquiry as to matters that may be relevant to employee fitness do not offend due process of law.

## ADLER v. BOARD OF EDUCATION, 342 U.S. 485 (1952)

**Facts:** A New York City Civil Service statute made any member of any organization which advocates the overthrow of the government by force or illegal means ineligible for employment in the public schools. A list of proscribed organizations was drawn up and membership in any organization on the list was, on its face, evidence of disqualification for employment in the public schools. However, no organization could be placed on the list without a hearing. Similarly, no person could be fired or denied employment on the basis of membership in an organization without a hearing. The decision reached at the hearing was then subject to review in the courts. If the employee could show that despite membership in a proscribed organization he was fit to be a teacher, the sanction would not be applied. The New York courts interpreted the law to require that membership in a proscribed organization be knowing, that is, that the member know the subversive nature of the organization he/she joins, before sanctions may be applied.

**Holding:** (7x3) A law disqualifying knowing members of proscribed organizations from employment in the public schools is constitutional where the presumption of unfitness to teach may be rebutted at a required hearing. Membership in such organizations is considered *prima facie* evidence for dismissal.

**Basis:** The Court finds the law to be sufficiently narrow for the Fourteenth Amendment's due process clause void-for-vagueness doctrine because it penalized only knowing membership and provides for a hearing. The Court finds no infringement of the First Amendment freedom of speech and assembly since it finds that employment in the public schools is not a right but a privilege which may be conditioned on reasonable state requirements.

## WIEMAN v. UPDEGRAFF, 344 U.S. 183 (1952)

*Facts:*  An Oklahoma statute required each state employee, as a condition of his employment, to take a "loyalty oath" stating that he is not and has not been for the preceding five years a member of any organization listed by the United States Attorney General as "communist front" or "subversive." Several employees of an Oklahoma state college failed to take the oath. Although the state supreme court interpreted the statute as limited to the list of prohibited organizations in existence at the time of the statute's enactment, it denied the employees' request that they be permitted to take the oath as so interpreted. The employees sought a declaration that the statute was unconstitutional and an order to require state officers to pay them regardless of their failure to take the oath.

*Holding:*  (5x3) It is unconstitutional for a statute to condition public employment on the taking of a loyalty oath based on innocent, as well as knowing, membership in a subversive organization.

*Bases:*  (1) The decision is based on the due process clause of the Fourteenth Amendment. To be valid under this clause, a statute must require that those to be penalized have actual knowledge of which organizations are banned and of the actual proscribed purpose of any organization to which they may belong. The Court states: "Indiscriminate classification of innocent with knowing activity must fall as an assertion of arbitrary power." The Court assumes that the oath penalizes innocent as well as knowing membership, since the employees' request to take the oath as limited by the state court's interpretation was refused by that court. (2) The Court also finds the statute to be an impermissible interference with the First Amendment freedom of association. To require such an oath, on pain of a teacher's loss of his/her position in case of his/her refusal to take the oath, penalizes a teacher for exercising his/her guaranteed right of association.

## SLOCHOWER v. BOARD OF HIGHER EDUCATION, 350 U.S. 551 (1956)

*Facts:*    Section 903 of the New York City Charter provided that a city employee who takes the Fifth Amendment before a legislative committee to avoid answering a question relating to his official conduct can be discharged from his/her job. A teacher in a city-operated college was discharged without notice or a hearing because he refused to answer a federal legislative committee's questions concerning his communist activities on the grounds that his answer might tend to incriminate him. The local board already possessed the information requested by the legislative committee. Under New York City law the teacher had tenure and could be discharged only for cause and only after having notice of the reasons, a hearing, and an opportunity for appeal. The teacher challenged the constitutionality of the termination of his employment under Section 903.

*Holding:*    (3/2x4) A board's action pursuant to a statute dismissing a teacher due to his/her refusal to answer questions irrelevant to an inquiry as to his/her fitness to teach and without a hearing is unconstitutional.

*Bases:*    (1) The due process clause of the Fourteenth Amendment protects the people from arbitrary state action. Since no inference of guilt can constitutionally be drawn from the taking of the Fifth Amendment and since the inquiry in question was unrelated to the board's search for information as to the employee's fitness to teach, the dismissal of the teacher was arbitrary and unconstitutional. (2) The Supreme Court does not find a constitutional right to public employment but follows *Wieman (supra)* in extending constitutional protection to a "public servant whose exclusion from such employment pursuant to a statute is patently arbitrary or discriminatory."

## BEILAN v. BOARD OF PUBLIC EDUCATION, 357 U.S. 399 (1958)

*Facts:*    A Philadelphia public school teacher refused to answer his superintendent's questions about his communist activities and affiliations. The teacher refused to answer even after the superintendent stressed that the purpose of the inquiry was to determine his fitness to teach and warned that his refusal to answer could result in dismissal. After a hearing at which the teacher's loyalty, political beliefs, and associations were not in

54

issue, the board of education found that the teacher's refusal to answer the superintendent's questions constituted "incompetency," grounds for discharge under state law, and discharged him. The teacher claimed that the board's action was unconstitutional.

*Holding:* (4/1x4) A board of education's discharge of a teacher for failure to respond to the superintendent's inquiry concerning his fitness to teach is in accord with the Constitution.

*Basis:* The school board may constitutionally inquire into an employee's fitness to teach, and such inquiry need not be limited to the employee's in-school activity. Such inquiry is not an infringement on the employee's First Amendment rights of freedom of speech, belief, or association.

## LERNER v. CASEY, 357 U. S. 468 (1958)

*Facts:* A subway conductor employed by the New York City Transit Authority was summoned to the office of Commissioner of Investigation of New York City and asked whether he was then a member of the Communist Party. He refused to answer and claimed his privilege against self-incrimination under the Fifth Amendment. Based upon his refusal, the City of New York found that his employment would endanger national and state security and suspended him. The conductor was later discharged after he failed to avail himself of an opportunity to submit statements showing why he should be reinstated. The conductor sued for reinstatement, alleging a violation of his constitutional right of due process.

*Holding:* (5/2x2) The discharge, pursuant to a state security law, of a public employee who refuses to answer questions relevant to his/her employment is constitutional.

*Basis:* The conductor's discharge was not based upon an inference of Communist Party membership drawn from the exercise of his Fifth Amendment privilege against self-incrimination, but rather upon a finding of "doubtful trust and reliability" resulting from his refusal to answer questions relevant to his employment put to him by his employer.

## SHELTON v. TUCKER, 364 U.S. 479 (1960)

*Facts:*    An Arkansas statute required every teacher, as a condition of employment in a state-supported school or college, to file an annual affidavit listing all organizations to which he/she has belonged or regularly contributed within the preceding five years. Teachers in the state school system had no tenure and were not covered by a civil service system. The statute thus required them to disclose the information to those who could fire them at will, without notice of the reasons or an opportunity for a hearing, at the end of any school year. In addition, the statute did not require that the information gathered be kept confidential. Teachers claimed that the statute unconstitutionally interfered with their personal, associational and academic freedom.

*Holding:*    (5x4) It is unconstitutional for a statute to require teachers in public schools and colleges, as a condition of employment, to list all organizations to which they have belonged or contributed in the past five years.

*Basis:*    The state has a right to investigate the fitness and competence of teachers, but the broad sweep of this statute interferes with associations that have no bearing on teacher fitness, goes far beyond what might be a legitimate inquiry, and thereby unconstitutionally impairs the teachers' right of freedom of association. This First Amendment right of freedom of association is protected from unnecessary or overbroad state interference by the due process clause of the Fourteenth Amendment. Limitation of the power of the states to interfere with personal freedoms of speech, inquiry, and association is especially important when those faced with impairment of rights are members of the academic community.

## CRAMP v. BOARD OF PUBLIC INSTRUCTION, 368 U.S. 278 (1961)

*Facts:*    A Florida statute required every employee of the state and its subdivisions to swear in writing that he/she has never lent his/her "aid, support, advice, counsel or influence to the Communist Party." It required the immediate discharge of any employee failing to take the oath. A teacher refused to subscribe to the oath and challenged the statute, claiming that its meaning was so vague as to deprive him of liberty. State courts interpreted the statute to apply only to acts done knowingly.

| | |
|---|---|
| *Holding:* | (7x2) A statute requiring state employees to swear that they never "knowingly lent their aid, support, advice, counsel or influence to the Communist Party" at the risk of prosecution for perjury or discharge from employment is unconstitutional. |
| *Basis:* | The law is so vague that it is difficult to determine what conduct is covered and what conduct is not. This vagueness violates the Fourteenth Amendment guarantee of due process of law. A statute is particularly scrutinized for vagueness when it operates, as it does here, to inhibit the exercise of freedoms affirmatively protected by the Constitution. |

## BAGGETT v. BULLITT, 377 U.S. 360 (1964)

| | |
|---|---|
| *Facts:* | Members of the faculty, staff, and student body of the University of Washington challenged the validity of two state statutes, passed in 1931 and 1955, which required the execution of two oaths as a condition of employment. The 1931 legislation, applicable only to teachers applying for a license to teach or renewing an existing contract, required such individuals to swear to "by precept and example . . . promote respect for the flag and the institutions of the United States . . . and the state of Washington, reverence for law and order, and undivided allegiance to the government of the United States." The 1955 legislation, applicable to all state employees, required each such individual to swear that he/she is not a "subversive person" and to disclaim membership in the Communist Party or any other subversive organization. He/she must, in taking this oath, affirm that he/she will not "commit, advise, teach, abet, or advocate another to commit or aid in the commission of any act intended to overthrow or alter, or assist in the overthrow or alteration, of the constitutional form of government by revolution, force, or violence." |
| *Holding:* | (7x2) Statutes which are so vaguely written that they could reasonably lead to prosecution for legally or constitutionally protected behavior are unconstitutional. |
| *Basis:* | While the power of a state to take proper steps to safeguard the public service from disloyal conduct is not denied, statutes which define disloyalty must not be vague in their terms and must allow public employees to know what is and what is not disloyal. In contrast, the 1931 and 1955 statutes and the oaths based on them required of employees are unduly vague, |

uncertain, and broad. Therefore, they are invalid under the due process clause of the Fourteenth Amendment. Vague language is especially susceptible to constitutional attack when it threatens to impair the exercise of First Amendment rights of freedom of speech and of association.

## ELFBRANDT v. RUSSELL, 384 U.S. 11 (1966)

*Facts:*    An Arizona act which required an oath from state employees was challenged by a teacher. She based her refusal on good conscience, claiming that the meaning of the oath was unclear and that she could not obtain a hearing in order to have the meaning determined. The oath reads:

> I do solemnly swear . . . that I will support the Constitution of the United States and . . . of the State of Arizona; that I will bear true faith and allegiance to the same, and defend them against all enemies, foreign and domestic, and that I will faithfully and impartially discharge the duties of the Office of (name of office) . . .

Anyone taking the oath was subject to prosecution for perjury and to discharge from office if he/she knowingly and willfully became or remained a member of the Communist Party or any other organization that advocated the overthrow of the government.

*Holding:*    (5x4) A loyalty oath statute which attaches sanctions to membership without requiring the "specific intent" to further the illegal aims of the organization is unconstitutional.

*Basis:*    The due process clause of the Fourteenth Amendment requires that a statute infringing on protected constitutional rights, in this case freedom of political association, be narrowly drawn to define and punish specific conduct constituting a clear and present danger to a substantial interest of the state. Those who join an organization without sharing in its unlawful purpose pose no threat to constitutional government.

## KEYISHIAN v. BOARD OF REGENTS, 385 U.S. 589 (1967)

New York had a complicated network of laws providing for the discharge of employees of the state educational system who utter "treasonable" or "seditious" words, do "treasonable" or "seditious" acts, who advocate or distribute written material in support of violent revolution, or who belong to "subversive" organizations. Faculty and staff members of the State University of New York, who refused to certify that they were not and had not been members of "subversive" organizations and who were therefore faced with discharge from their jobs, sought to have the New York teacher loyalty laws and regulations declared unconstitutional.

*Holding:* (5x5) Loyalty oath statutes which make membership in an organization, as such, sufficient for termination of employment are unconstitutional. To be valid, a loyalty law must be limited to knowing, active members who help to pursue the illegal goals of the subversive organization. In contrast, the New York laws are overbroad.

*Basis:* The opinion is based on the First Amendment freedoms of speech and association. The Court gives this safeguard particular importance when the issue involved is academic freedom.

## WHITEHILL v. ELKINS, 389 U.S. 54 (1967)

*Facts:* A teacher who was offered a position at the University of Maryland refused to take an oath certifying that he was not "engaged in one way or another in the attempt to overthrow the Government . . . by force or violence." The oath was part of a statutorily mandated procedure for determining whether a prospective employee is a "subversive." The term "subversive" is defined by Maryland statutes to include one who is a member of an organization which would alter, overthrow, or destroy the Government by revolution, force, or violence. The teacher challenged the validity of the oath.

*Holding:* (6x3) A statutorily prescribed loyalty oath conditioning public employment on mere membership in a subversive organization is unconstitutional.

*Basis:* First Amendment freedoms of speech and association are infringed by the oath's lack of clarity since it may be read to proscribe mere passive, as well as knowing, membership in an organization and support of peaceful, as well as violent, revolution. The due process clause of the Fourteenth Amendment prohibits such infringement. In addition, due process of law does not allow prosecution for perjury to rest on an unclear oath.

## PICKERING v. BOARD OF EDUCATION, 391 U.S. 563 (1968)

*Facts:*      The board of education dismissed a teacher for writing and sending to a newspaper for publication a letter criticizing the board's allocation of school funds between educational and athletic programs and the board's way of informing, or not informing, the public of the "real" reasons why additional tax revenues were being sought for schools. The dismissal resulted from a determination by the board, after a full hearing, that the publication of the letter was "detrimental to the efficient operation and administration of the schools of the district" and that, therefore, under the relevant Illinois statute, the "interest of the school required [his dismissal]." Some of the statements in the teacher's letter were substantially true. Others were false, but seemed to be the product of faulty research rather than being knowingly, maliciously, or recklessly false. The teacher challenged the constitutionality of this dismissal.

*Holding:*    (7/2x0) Absent proof of false statements knowingly or recklessly made by him/her, a teacher's exercise of his/her right to speak on issues of public importance, e.g., on the raising and disbursement of funds for education, may not be the basis of his/her dismissal from public employment. In this case, the dismissal of the teacher is improper.

*Bases:*      (1) The teacher's First Amendment right to freedom of expression is balanced against the state interest in efficient public schools. Where a teacher's comments deal with a matter of public interest and do not impair the day-to-day operation of the schools or the performance of duties, dismissal based on such comments is violative of First Amendment rights since the teacher is entitled to the same protection under that Amendment as any member of the general public would have. (2) The Court does not decide whether a statement that was knowingly or recklessly false would, if *not* proven to have harmful effects, still be protected by the First Amendment.

## MARYLAND v. WIRTZ, 392 U.S. 183 (1968)*

*Facts:*      The Fair Labor Standards Act of 1938 requires every employer to pay each of his employees "engaged in commerce or in the production of goods for commerce" certain minimum wages and overtime pay. The original Act's definition of "employer"

*Reversed by *National League of Cities v. Usery infra.*

excluded the federal and state governments. In 1961, the Act's coverage was extended beyond employees directly connected with interstate commerce to include all employees of enterprises engaged in commerce or in production for commerce. In 1966, the Act's definition of "employer" was modified so as to remove the exemption for states and their subdivisions with respect to employees of hospitals, institutions, and schools. In this case, 28 states and a school district challenged the validity of these amendments.

*Holding:*   (7x2) The 1961 and 1966 amendments to the Fair Labor Standards Act, which extend the Act's application *inter alia,* to school employees, are constitutional.

*Basis:*   The Court finds the Act and its "enterprise" concept to be clearly within the power of Congress under the commerce clause. It is a rational regulation of activities which have a substantial effect on interstate commerce and on national labor conditions. The amount of Congressional interference is minimal, extending only to wages and hours. The argument that the Tenth Amendment prohibits such interference with the states is rejected by the majority.

## EPPERSON v. ARKANSAS, 393 U.S. 97 (1968)

*Facts:*   A 1928 Arkansas statute prohibited teachers in any state supported school from teaching the Darwinian theory of the evolution of man. Violators faced dismissal from their jobs. The biology text provided for the 1965-66 school year at a high school in Little Rock contained a chapter on the proscribed theory. In this case, a teacher at the high school sought to have the statute invalidated so that she could include the chapter on evolution in her program of instruction.

*Holding:*   (6/3x0) A law forbidding the teaching of the Darwinian theory of the evolution of man is unconstitutional.

*Basis:*   The statute violates the First Amendment's prohibition of state establishment of religion as incorporated through the Fourteenth Amendment. The purpose of the statute was not to excise all discussion of evolution from the curriculum but to proscribe a discussion of the subject which was considered by a religious group to be in conflict with the Bible. Such state action is not within the bounds of neutrality towards religion required by the First Amendment.

61

## CONNELL v. HIGGINBOTHAM, 403 U.S. 207 (1971)

*Facts:*  A teacher was dismissed for her failure to sign a loyalty oath which stated the following: I do hereby solemnly swear "that I will support the Constitution of the United States and of the State of Florida;" and "that I do not believe in the overthrow of the Government of the United States or of the State of Florida by force or violence." She challenged the constitutionality of the two clauses.

*Holding:*  (5/3½x½) (1) A loyalty oath provision conditioning public employment on the employee's required affirmation that he/she will support the federal and state constitutions is valid. (2) A provision requiring a public employee(s) to swear that he/she does not believe in the violent overthrow of the federal or state government is invalid where it provides for dismissal without a hearing.

*Bases:*  (1) Oaths which are prospectively promissory, and which do not require specific future acts, are not unconstitutional infringements on First Amendment rights of freedom of speech and association. (2) The majority finds that mere refusal to take the oath is not irrebuttable proof of unfitness to teach. Thus, the statute's provision for dismissal without a hearing offends the due process clause of the Fourteenth Amendment. The concurring opinion would invalidate this clause on First Amendment grounds, that is, that one may not be penalized for a belief per se.

## COLE v. RICHARDSON, 405 U.S. 676 (1972)

*Facts:*  In Massachusetts a public employee was discharged because she refused to subscribe to the following loyalty oath:

> I do solemnly swear . . . that *I will* uphold and defend the Constitution of the United States . . . and the Constitution of the Commonwealth of Massachusetts and that *I will* oppose the overthrow of the government of the United States or this Commonwealth by force, violence or by any illegal or unconstitutional method. (emphasis added)

The employee claimed that the oath is unconstitutional and sought to have its application enjoined.

*Holding:*  (2/2x3) (1) A loyalty oath required for public employment which is addressed to future rather than to past conduct and

62

which speaks in general rather than in specific terms is constitutional. (2) An employee refusing to take a constitutional oath has no right to a hearing prior to discharge from employment.

*Bases:* (1) The First Amendment freedoms of speech and association are not impaired by the oath since it does not bar past, present, or future membership in any organization or past expressions of opinion or belief. The Court finds the oath to not require that specific action be taken in a future actual or hypothetical situation but rather to be "simply an acknowledgement of a willingness to abide by constitutional processes of government." (2) Fourteenth Amendment due process protection of a hearing prior to discharge from employment is not required since there is no constitutionally protected right to overthrow the government by unconstitutional means and the oath is merely an expression of a commitment to live by the constitutitonal processes of our system of government.

## BOARD OF REGENTS v. ROTH, 408 U.S. 564 (1972)

*Facts:* A teacher was hired by a state university for a fixed term of one academic year and was later notified that he would not be rehired for the following year. State law, university regulations, and the teacher's contract did not provide for a pretermination hearing or require that reasons for dismissal be given to a nontenured teacher whose employment was terminated at the end of an academic year. In this case, the teacher challenged the constitutionality of the state university's action in dismissing him without notice of the reasons for its decision and without a hearing.

*Holding:* (5x3) The state may properly fail to rehire a nontenured teacher at the end of a fixed period of employment without providing such an employee with the reasons for the decision or with a pretermination hearing.

*Bases:* The Fourteenth Amendment mandates that state action impairing a person's life, liberty, or property interest meet the requirement of due process of law. If, as in this case, no life, liberty, or property interest is impaired, no due process of law is required by the Fourteenth Amendment. (1) The Court finds that a nontenured teacher who is not rehired at the end of an academic year is, absent any employer's statement that would

63

damage his reputation, free to seek other employment. A person is not deprived of "liberty"* protected by the Fourteenth Amendment when he/she simply is not rehired in one job and remains as free as before to seek another. (2) The Court finds that no state law, university policy, or term of the employment contract contains language creating an entilement or expectation of continued employment. A teacher has no constitutionally protected "property" interest in continued employment, absent any statutory or administrative standards granting eligibility for reemployment. (3) The Court did not decide whether the teacher had been fired for speech protected by the First Amendment.

## PERRY v. SINDERMANN, 408 U.S. 593 (1972)

*Facts:*      A teacher in the state college system, who had been employed for ten years under a series of one-year contracts and who was without formal tenure rights, was fired after he had publicly criticized the policies of the Board of Regents. The regents issued a press release stating that insubordination was the reason for dismissal but provided the teacher with no official statement of reasons. There was no pretermination hearing. The teacher challenged the validity of the regents' termination of his employment, claiming that their decision was unconstitutionally based on his expressions of opinion on matters of public concern and was also invalid for failing to accord him the right to a pretermination hearing. Although he had no formal tenured or contractual interest in being rehired, he relied on *de facto* tenure based on language in the college's official Faculty Guide and in the guidelines promulgated for the Texas College and University System. The guidelines provide that a teacher with seven years of employment in the system is tenured and can only be dismissed for cause.

*Holding:*      (6½x1½) (1) A teacher's public criticism of his/her superiors on matters of public concern is constitutionally protected and may not be the basis for termination of employment. This right not to be discharged for constitutionally protected conduct does not depend on the presence or absence of tenure rights. (2) A teacher's subjective expectation of tenure will not require the administration to provide reasons and pretermination hearing at which the sufficiency of those reasons may be challenged. However, an objective expectation of reemployment, for

*For subsequent Supreme Court cases which delineate the "liberty" interest see *Bishop v. Wood infra* and *Paul v. Davis,* 424 U.S. 693 (1976).

example arising from rules and understandings officially fostered and promulgated by the public employer, will require that such procedural safeguards precede termination of employment.

*Bases:* (1) The First Amendment, made applicable to the states through the Fourteenth Amendment, prohibits state action which impairs freedom of speech and expression. A person may not be denied a governmental benefit because of the exercise of constitutionally protected rights. (2) An objective expectation of tenure creates a "property" interest in continued employment which is protected by the due process clause of the Fourteenth Amendment. The state may not impair a life, liberty, or property interest arbitrarily or without affording the injured party appropriate procedural protections.

## GEDULDIG v. AIELLO, 417 U.S. 484 (1974)

*Facts:* California has a disability insurance plan for private employees temporarily disabled by an injury or illness that is not covered by Workmen's Compensation. Employees contribute 1% of their salary up to an annual maximum amount, and the program is compulsory unless suitable private insurance is substituted. The plan's coverage is not comprehensive and certain disabilities are excluded. Among the conditions which are not compensable is disability resulting from a normal pregnancy. This exclusion was challenged here.

*Holding:* (6x3) The exclusion of disability arising in a normal pregnancy from eligibility for benefits under a state-run insurance program is constitutional.

*Basis:* Since the exclusion of disability arising in normal pregnancy is not sex-based discrimination, it is not barred by the equal protection clause of the Fourteenth Amendment. Also, the equal protection clause does not require the state to compensate all disabilities or none. The legislature may attempt to ameliorate part of a problem without attacking the whole and, absent invidious discrimination, its action will pass the constitutional test. The state's insurance plan is designed to provide minimally adequate coverage affordable by even low-income groups. The inclusion of benefits for normal pregnancy would force major alteration of this reasonable program and is not required.

## MCCARTHY v. PHILADELPHIA CIVIL SERVICE COMMISSION, 424 U.S. 645 (1976)

*Facts:*  After sixteen years of service, a fireman was discharged because he moved his permanent residence from Philadelphia to New Jersey. A Philadelphia municipal ordinance required employees of the city to reside in Philadelphia. The fireman challenged the constitutionality of the ordinance under which he was discharged.

*Holding:*  (*per curiam* 6/3x0) An ordinance may properly require city employees to reside in the city at the time of their application for employment and as a condition of continued employment.

*Bases:*  There is a federally protected right to interstate travel but this right is not infringed by laws requiring prior residency of a certain duration as a condition of eligibility and not by laws containing present and continuing residency requirement. The status of city employees who resided outside of the city at the time of the ordinance's effective date was not at issue in this case.

## BISHOP v. WOOD, 426 U.S. 341 (1976)

*Facts:*  A permanently employed policeman was discharged without a hearing. He was told that the dismissal was based on his failure to perform his duties adequately and on conduct unsuited to an officer. A city ordinance provides that a permanent employee be given notice if his/her work is deficient so that he/she may have an opportunity to bring his/her performance up to a satisfactory level. It provides for dismissal for cause. There is no statutory provision for a pretermination hearing but, upon request, a terminated permanent employee is entitled to notice of the reasons for discharge. The policeman claimed a constitutional right to a pretermination hearing.

*Holding:*  (5 x 4) Where according to state court decisions, there is no statutory or contractural entitlement to continued employment and where the reasons for discharge, although damaging to the employee's reputation, are not made public, there is no constitutional right to a pretermination hearing.

*Bases:*  In order to be protected by the due process clause of the Fourteenth Amendment, an employee facing discharge must also face impairment of a liberty or property interest by the state's termination of his employment. (1) Where the state court and local federal court decisions indicate that there is no entitlement to or expectation of continued employment such as is protected by the Fourteenth Amendment, the Court will not find a constitutionally protected property interest requiring a pretermination hearing. (2) Where the reasons for discharge, although damaging to the employee, are not made public, there is no harm done to the employee's reputation and his/her ability to find other employment is unimpaired. His/her liberty interest under the Fourteenth Amendment is not infringed.

## HORTONVILLE JOINT SCHOOL DISTRICT NO. 1 v. HORTONVILLE EDUCATION ASSOCIATION, 426 U.S. 482 (1976)

*Facts:* Prolonged negotiations between teachers and a Wisconsin school board failed to produce a contract and the teachers went on strike. Under state law the board has the power to negotiate terms of employment with teachers and is the only body vested by statute with the power to employ and dismiss teachers. There is no statute providing for review of board decisions on such matters. However, there is a statutory prohibition against teacher strikes. The teachers refused repeated board urgings that they return to work. The board then held a hearing for the striking teachers and voted to terminate their employment. The teachers contended that they have been denied due process of law required by the Fourteenth Amendment because they were discharged by the school board, a decision-making body that they claimed was not impartial.

*Holding:* (6x3) Absent a showing of bias or malice, a local school board can validly conduct a hearing to terminate illegally striking teachers even though the board was negotiating labor questions with the teachers.

*Basis:* Using a balancing approach, the Court defers to the state's interest in maintaining the allocation of responsibility for school matters that is established by statute. Where there is no showing of personal, financial, or anti-union bias, the presumption that the school board will fulfill the Fourteenth Amendment due process requirement of impartiality stands.

67

# NATIONAL LEAGUE OF CITIES v. USERY, 426 U.S. 833 (1976)

*Facts:*    The original Fair Labor Standards Act of 1938 specifically excluded the states from its coverage. In 1966, the definition of "employer" under the Act was extended to include the state governments with respect to employees of state hospitals, institutions, and schools. This extension was upheld by the Supreme Court in *Maryland* v. *Wirtz, (supra).* In 1974, the Act was amended so as to extend its minimum wage and maximum hours to almost all employees of the states and their political subdivisions. In this case, a number of cities and states challenged the validity of these amendments.

*Holding:*    (4/1x4) The 1966 and 1974 amendments to the Fair Labor Standards Act are unconstitutional. *Maryland* v. *Wirtz (supra)* is overruled.

*Basis:*    In the absence of a national emergency, the Tenth Amendment forbids Congress to exercise power in a fashion that impairs the integrity of the states as governmental units or their ability to function in a federal system. The Fair Labor Standards Act as amended in 1966 and 1974 infringes on the states' sovereignty by attempting to prescribe minimum wages and maximum salaries for state employees performing traditional governmental functions.

# MASSACHUSETTS BOARD OF RETIREMENT v. MURGIA, 427 U.S. 307 (1976)*

*Facts:*    A state statute requires that uniformed state police officers be retired when they reach age fifty. In accord with this statute, a 50-year old officer was retired although he was still physically capable of doing his job and did not wish to retire. He challenged the constitutionality of the statute.

*Holding:*    (7x1) The law requiring state police officers to retire at age fifty is constitutional.

*Basis:*    The policeman claims that the law denies him equal protection of the laws guaranteed by the Fourteenth Amendment, To be constitutional, the state's forced retirement of 50-year-old policemen need only be rationally related to a legitimate state

---

*For a recent related case, based on statutory construction, see *United Airlines* v. *McMann,* 46 U.S.L.W. 4043 (Dec. 13, 1977).

purpose. A test more protective of the employees' rights would be used by the courts if employment as an officer were a fundamental right or if classifications based on age fifty were discriminatory against a minority group historically mistreated and therefore in need of extra protection. Age groups are not considered such a class. (Racial and national origin minority groups, for example, are afforded extra protection.) Since police work is physically demanding and since physical prowess diminishes with advancing age, the state regulation is rational. The state's decision not to do more individualized assessments of physical ability may not be wise, but it is not unconstitutional.

## MADISON v. WISCONSIN EMPLOYMENT RELATIONS COMMISSION, 429 U.S. 167 (1976)

*Facts:*    In 1971, the Board of Education and the teacher's union, the exclusive bargaining agent, were negotiating a collective bargaining agreement. One issue under discussion was the union's demand for a "fair share" clause requiring all teachers within the bargaining unit to pay union dues, whether or not they were union members. Wisconsin had a law prohibiting school boards from negotiating with individual teachers once an exclusive bargaining agent has been elected.

During an open public meeting held by the school board, a teacher who was not a representative of the union spoke briefly, urging that a decision on the "fair share" clause be delayed until the matter was studied by an impartial committee and until the teachers and the public were properly informed about the issue. The State Employment Relations Committee found the board guilty of the prohibited practice of negotiating with a party other than the exclusive bargaining agent and ordered that the board cease to permit any employees but union officials to speak at board meetings on matters subject to collective bargaining. The school board challenged this ruling.

*Holding:*    (6/2/1x0) A State Employment Commission order prohibiting the public school board from allowing teachers who are not union representatives to speak during public meetings, if the matter they wish to discuss is subject to collective bargaining, is unconstitutional.

*Bases:*    (1) The teachers have a First Amendment right to communicate with the board. When the board holds a public meeting in order

69

to hear the views of the people, it may not be required to infringe on the First Amendment rights of some part of the public on the basis of employment or of the content of speech. (2) The non-union teacher's brief statement was a concerned citizen's expression of public opinion and not an attempt to negotiate with the board. The union remained the sole and unchallenged collective bargaining agent. The teacher's First Amendment freedom of speech could not reasonably be curtailed as a danger to labor-management relations.

## MOUNT HEALTHY CITY SCHOOL DISTRICT v. DOYLE, 97 S. Ct. 568 (1977)

*Facts:* A nontenured teacher, who had previously been involved in several altercations with other teachers, employees, and students, including an incident in which he made obscene gestures to female students, phoned in to a radio station the substance of the school principal's memorandum to faculty concerning a teacher dress code. The radio station announced the adoption of the dress code as a news item. Thereafter, the school board, on the recommendation of the superintendent, told the teacher he would not be rehired. The board cited the teacher's lack of tact in handling professional matters and mentioned specifically the obscene gesture and radio station incidents. The teacher challenged the validity of the termination of his employment based on the above-mentioned grounds.

*Holding:* (9x0) (1) The teacher's call to the radio station was constitutionally protected speech and was a substantial or motivating factor in the school board's decision to terminate his employment. (2) If the teacher's employment would not have been terminated but for his protected conduct, then he is entitled to reinstatement and to back pay. If the teacher would have been dismissed even if he had not done the constitutionally protected act, then the school board is not required to retain him and termination of his employment is acceptable. (3) Once the teacher shows that his constitutionally protected conduct was a substantial factor in the board's decision not to rehire him, the board in order to successfully defend its decision must show by a preponderance of the evidence that it would have reached that same decision even in the absence of the protected conduct.

70

**Basis:** The First Amendment, made applicable to the states by the Fourteenth Amendment, protects the teacher's right to freedom of speech. Since the teacher's conduct did not disrupt the orderly operation of the school, it was constitutionally protected and could not serve as the basis for the termination of his/her employment. However, the teacher should not be able by engaging in "constitutionally protected conduct" to prevent an employer from assessing his/her entire performance record and reach a decision not to rehire on the basis of that record.

## CODD v. VELGER, 97 S. Ct. 882 (1977)

**Facts:** Police officer Velger was dismissed from employment during his probationary training period because he put a revolver to his head in an apparent suicide attempt. This information was placed in a file which a later employer examined with Velger's permission. Velger was dismissed from his second job and was refused several others as well. Velger was not afforded a hearing prior to his dismissals. He claimed that the city's failure to provide him with a hearing entitled him to reinstatement and to money damages. He did not claim that the statement in the file was untrue.

**Holding:** (per curiam 4/1x4) A dismissed nontenured employee claiming that his/her reputation and chances for future employment have been impaired by information placed in his/her file and seeking reinstatement and damages because he/she was not afforded a pretermination hearing must allege that the prejudicial information contained in the file is false. In the absence of such an assertion, his/her claims fails.

**Basis:** The due process clause of the Fourteenth Amendment protects a person's liberty interest in his/her good name and continued prospects for employment. Therefore, even a nontenured employee is entitled to a hearing prior to termination if the employer creates and disseminates a false and defamatory impression about the employee and the reasons for dismissal. If a tenured employee does not assert that the information disseminated is false, then he/she cannot assert a claim for damages arising from the lack of a hearing. A hearing would be of no use to a person in an attempt to clear his/her name as he/she would be unable to refute the information in the file.

71

## ABOOD v. DETROIT BOARD OF EDUCATION, 45 U.S.L.W. 4473 (May 23, 1977)

*Facts:*    Michigan legislation authorized a system for union representation of employees of local governmental units. It specifically permits a union and a local government employer to agree on an "agency shop" arrangement by which each employee represented by the union must pay the union dues or, if he/she is not a union member, an equivalent amount. An employee who fails to comply faces discharge from employment. The authorized teachers' union for employees of the Detroit Board of Education is the Detroit Federation of Teachers. In 1969, this union entered into an "agency shop" agreement with the Board. In this case, teachers who are opposed to collective bargaining for public employees challenged the constitutionality of the agreement which forces them to support the union's collective activities. They also challenged the allocation of part of their money to the support of a variety of union activities that are economic, political, professional, or religious in nature and not directly related to the union's collective bargaining function.

*Holding:*    (6/3x0) (1) Local governmental employment may properly be conditioned on an employee's payment of union dues or their equivalent when such funds are used by the union for collective bargaining, contract administration, and grievance adjustment purposes. (2) However, the Constitution requires that funds paid by employees as a condition of continued government employment not be used by the union for ideological, political purposes which are not directly related to its collective bargaining function.

*Basis:*    The First Amendment guarantees of speech and belief, made applicable to the states by the Fourteenth Amendment, forbids that public employment be conditioned on the payment of union dues which are used to force ideological conformity or support of a political position.

## INTERNATIONAL BROTHERHOOD OF TEAMSTERS v. UNITED STATES, 45 U.S.L.W. 4506 (May 23, 1977)

*Facts:*    The Federal Government brought this action under Title VII of the Civil Rights Act of 1964 which prohibits discrimination in employment. The Government claimed that a large carrier of motor freight had discriminated against minority group members by hiring them only as local city drivers while reserving the higher paying, long distance line drives jobs for whites. The Government further claimed that the seniority system agreed upon by the Teamster's Union and the employer perpetuated the effects of this past discrimination since under that system a city driver transferring to a long distance line driver job had to forfeit all his city driver seniority and start at the bottom of line drivers' "board." The Government sought a court order permitting city drivers to transfer to line driver status with full seniority.

*Holding:* (7/1x1) The Government sustained its burden of proving that the company engaged in a system-wide pattern or practice of employment discrimination against minority members in violation of Title VII. Employees who, after the effective date of Title VII, either were denied jobs because of racial or ethnic discrimination or who were deterred from applying for such jobs because of the company's known discrimination policy, are entitled to retroactive seniority dating back to no later than the effective date of the Act. Employees who suffered only pre-Act discrimination are not entitled to relief.

*Basis:* Seniority systems in a bargaining agreement may perpetuate the effects of past racial and ethnic discrimination. Lower paid employees, if made to forfeit their seniority in order to transfer to a higher paid job, may show that the company is engaged in a practice violative of the Civil Rights Act of 1964.

# V. RACE, LANGUAGE, AND SEX
# DISCRIMINATION

*Reviewer:* David G. Carter
Associate Dean
School of Education
University of Connecticut

This chapter focuses on Supreme Court cases in the area of race, sex, and language discrimination. A review of these will reveal the range of issues which has emerged as a result of the numerous court decisions. The Court, through rendering a variety of decisions concerning discrimination, has charted a somewhat meandering course.

It provides some perspective, if little comfort, to recall that resistance to segregation as a significant link in the move toward integration did not commence in 1954 with the *Brown I* decision, but weaves through the historic fabric of this country. In retrospect one sees that when the Supreme Court ruled that segregation of school children on the basis of race was unconstitutional, the Constitution changed much more significantly than the schools. In practice, the decision failed, as *Brown II* (1955) did, to inspire reform in the schools "with all deliberate speed."

During the year following *Brown II,* the Supreme Court refrained from active involvement in the desegregation process; rather it relied on the lower courts to bring about desegregation process "with all deliberate speed." But concerned with the slow rate of progress, the Court, on May 27, 1968, rendered its *Green v. County School Board* decision, and set the stage for a new era in school desegregation. This ruling brought to an end the so-called "freedom of choice" options as the predominant means of implementing desegregation because they had utterly failed to bring about desegregation in the South.

Although the Court did not rule in *Green* that freedom of choice plans were unconstitutional, it did state "the burden on a school board today is to come forward with a plan that promises realistically to work, and promises realistically to work now." The criterion used to determine success was the existence of a plan to achieve desegregation.

The Court went on to say that if other reasonable ways to bring about a "unitary, nonracial school system exist, freedom of choice must be held unacceptable." Therefore, the school board was directed to take steps that would change "black" and "white" schools into schools without those adjectives.

It was in *Green* that the Court first adopted the percentage of black-white students attending a given school as the primary measurement of whether a desegregation plan had been effective in achieving a unitary, nonracial school system. But instead of reducing the number of desegregation cases, the *Green* decision actually increased the litigation as school systems began to avail themselves of the apparent loopholes left by that decision. These loopholes included the failure of the Court to define what a working desegregation plan would entail and the failure to specify what a unitary school system was. The ambiguity surrounding these two points generated confusion and further litigation.

It was not until June 29, 1970, when the Supreme Court granted *certiorari* that some of the complex problems raised in earlier decisions on busing were addressed. Federal District Court Judge James McMillan of Charlotte, North Carolina, in *Swann v. Charlotte-Mecklenburg Board of Education*, had rendered a decision supporting racial balancing that necessitated busing school children in metropolitan Charlotte and Mecklenburg County.

When the Supreme Court granted *certiorari* in the *Swann* case, school districts everywhere waited anxiously for its decision. While the case was under consideration, the federal courts operated without definite direction to the extent to which busing could be used to effect desegregation. In its decision, the Supreme Court considered for the first time corrective steps that a District Court could take in ordering a public school system to cease functioning as a segregated system. In a unanimous opinion the Court discussed and approved several remedies and specifically upheld the transporting included in Judge McMillan's order. The Supreme Court entered only one stipulation: "An objection to transportation of students may have validity when the time or distance of travel is so great as to risk either the health of the children or significantly impinge on the educational process." The court discussed these "transportation limitations" as follows: "Limits on time of travel will vary with many factors, but probably none more than the age of the students." The Supreme Court Justices noted that bus transportation had been an "integral part of the public education system for years and was perhaps the single most important factor in the transition from the one-room school house to the consolidated school. In 1976, 43% of all school students were bused, but only 4% of them were bused for desegregation purposes.

Reaction concerning the Supreme Court's ruling in *Swann* came quickly, and those opposing busing proposed a number of alternate means for limiting or eliminating it. Both Congress and the Executive branch have, in general, resisted court-ordered desegregation involving busing since the *Swann* decision.

While *Swann* can be viewed as being representative of *de jure* cases, the

75

Supreme Court's involvement with a school system where segregation had never been law, but segregated schools existed nonetheless (*de facto*), came about in *Keyes v. School District No. 1, Denver. Colorado* (1973). This case is significant for two additional reasons. First, it sought to eliminate segregation by crossing school district boundaries which involved an increase in court-ordered transportation of students. Next, the Court required the desegregation plan to reflect the bilingual-bicultural needs of Hispano-Americans. By contrast, in 1974, when the Supreme Court heard arguments on the *Milliken v. Bradley* case, the majority and dissenting justices agreed that the actions of the Detroit School Board and the State of Michigan contributed to the perpetuation of segregation. However, since no basis was established concerning inter-district violation of desegregation efforts, a remedy requiring inter-district participation was "unsupported by record evidence."

Another aspect of discrimination emerged when the Court heard *Lau v. Nichols.* This case and others moved beyond the melting pot notion of racial integration and moved toward the idea that schools must adapt to meet the language and other needs of the students.

Sex discrimination represents the most recent area with which the Court has become increasingly involved. Although the cases in this area are few, it appears to be an area of increasing litigation.

The contemporary judicial landscape is cluttered with decrees, many of which are enmeshed in controversy. False liability and remedy quests persist and new issues emerge as more court rulings are decided. Each case concerning discrimination must be interpreted within the limited context of the specific facts of that case. This is not to say that principles of law have not been established, only that the complexity of each case is such that it must be viewed individually.

The one constant which can be found in all of the cases reviewed is the courts unwavering support of justice. However, because judicial decisions frequently raise a number of questions, speculation as to the future of discrimination efforts by the Court should be made with caution.

## PLESSY v. FERGUSON, 163 U.S. 537 (1896)*

*Facts:* A man who was a citizen of the United States and a resident of Louisiana challenged a Louisiana law which required railway companies to provide separate-but-equal facilities to whites and to blacks and which provided criminal penalties for passengers who insisted on being seated in a car not reserved for their own race.

*Holding:* (7x1) The law requiring segregation of the races in railway cars

*Reversed by *Brown v. Board of Education ("Brown I")* infra.*

76

and providing for separate-but-equal facilities for both whites and blacks is constitutional.

*Bases:* (1) The Thirteenth Amendment abolished slavery but is not a bar to actions short of involuntary servitude which may nevertheless burden the black race. (2) The Fourteenth Amendment prohibits the state from making any law which impairs the life, liberty, or property interest of any person under the jurisdiction of the United States. Although this Amendment requires equality between the races before the law, it does not require the social comingling of the races or the abolition of social distinctions based on skin color.

## CUMMING v. RICHMOND COUNTY BOARD OF EDUCATION, 175 U.S. 528 (1899)

*Facts:* A state law required the provision of separate-but-equal public educational facilities to children of both races. However, the local school board ceased operation of the high school which served sixty black students, while continuing to support a high school for white girls and to aid a high school for white boys. The school board claimed their action was caused not by hostility toward blacks but by a lack of funds which obliged a choice between an elementary school for blacks or a high school for blacks.

*Holding:* (9x0) It is constitutionally permissible for a school district to provide a high school education for white children but not for black children where the reason is lack of funds rather than hostility toward the black race.

*Basis:* Absent the state's clear and unmistakable disregard of rights secured by the Constitution, federal interference with a state program of public education cannot be justified. The board's action in closing the black high school for lack of funds was not an arbitrary denial of equal treatment under the law such as is prohibited by the equal protection clause of the Fourteenth Amendment.

## FARRINGTON v. TOKUSHIGE, 273 U.S. 284 (1927)

*Facts:* Numerous private Japanese language schools challenged as unconstitutional a Hawaiian statute which required schools conducted in languages other than English or Hawaiian to

77

obtain a written permit and to pay an annual fee of $1.00 per pupil to the Department of Public Instruction. Other sections of the statute limited the hours of instruction, the subjects taught, and texts used. The statute also required that students reach a certain age and level of academic achievement before being permitted to attend a foreign language school.

*Holding:* (9x0) A state law which gives affirmative directions concerning the intimate and essential details of private schools and which entrusts their control to public officers and denies both owners and patrons reasonable choice and discretion with respect to teachers, curriculum, and texts is unconstitutional.

*Bases:* The Fifth Amendment provides that no person shall be deprived of life, liberty, or property without due process of law and applies to the federal government and to the governments of federal territories. (1) The pervasive regulation of private schools mandated by the statute in question infringes on the property interests of the foreign language schools since it would probably destroy most of them. (2) The statute infringes on the liberty interests of parents who wish their children to be instructed in a foreign language since it severely burdens and limits such instruction. (3) The statute cannot be justified by an overriding public interest and is therefore an unreasonable infringement on property and liberty interests in violation of the Fifth Amendment.

## GONG LUM v. RICE, 275 U.S. 78 (1927)

*Facts:* The superintendent of education of Mississippi excluded Gong Lum's daughter from attending a white school because she was not a member of the white race. The superintendent was acting pursuant to the state constitutional provision which states: "[S]eparate schools shall be maintained for children of the white and colored races."

*Holding:* (9x0) No right of a Chinese citizen is infringed by classifying him/her for purposes of education with black children and denying him/her the right to attend schools established for the white race.

*Basis:* A state may regulate the method of providing for the education of its youth at public expense. The establishment of separate schools for white and black students is permitted. The separation between white and yellow students is not treated differently. The decision to place Chinese students in the black schools is within the state's authority to regulate its public schools and does not conflict with the Fourteenth Amendment.

## SWEATT v. PAINTER, 339 U.S. 629 (1950)

*Facts:*  A black student was denied admission to the state-supported University of Texas Law School solely on the basis of race. State law prohibited the admission of blacks to the university of which the law school was a part. Under a court order to afford the student a legal education, Texas created a separate law school for blacks. The new school was not the equal of the university law school in many respects ranging from size to such intangible qualities as reputation of faculty and alumni, standing in the community, traditions, and prestige. In addition, the black law school could not enroll whites. The black student refused to enroll in the new law school and here sought entry into the university law school.

*Holding:*  (9x0) The legal education offered to the black student by the state is not substantially equal to that which he would receive if admitted to the University of Texas Law School and, if qualified, the student must be admitted to the University of Texas Law School.

*Basis:*  The equal protection clause of the Fourteenth Amendment prohibits state action which discriminates against persons on the basis of race. The law school education offered to blacks by Texas is inferior to that offered to whites in many tangible and intangible ways. These considerations make it mandatory that Texas admit blacks to its previously all-white law school.

## MCLAURIN v. OKLAHOMA STATE REGENTS FOR HIGHER EDUCATION, 339 U.S. 637 (1950)

*Facts:*  A black citizen of Oklahoma was admitted to the graduate school of the state university as a doctoral candidate. A state law required that blacks be admitted to white educational programs only when comparable programs were unavailable at black state colleges and that their education was to continue on a segregated basis. In accord with this law, the student was assigned isolated seats in the classrooms, library, and cafeteria.

In this case, he challenged the constitutionality of the restrictions on his university attendance.

*Holding:* (9x0) A student admitted to a state graduate school must receive equal treatment. The state may not discriminate against students on a racial basis by isolating minority group students from the majority of the student body.

*Basis:* The Fourteenth Amendment prohibits state action which arbitrarily denies a person or group equal protection of the law. The restrictions imposed on the student because of his race impair his ability to pursue his education and deny him equal protection of the law.

## BROWN v. BOARD OF EDUCATION, 347 U.S. 483 (1954) *("Brown I")*

*Facts:* Four separate cases from the states of Kansas, South Carolina, Virginia, and Delaware were consolidated and decided in this case. In each of the cases, black students sought admission to the public schools of their community on a non-segregated basis. Kansas, by state law, permitted but did not require segregated schools. South Carolina, Virginia, and Delaware had state constitutional and statutory provisions which required the segregation of blacks and whites in public schools. State residents and taxpayers who were challenging these laws were denied relief, except in the Delaware case. The courts denying relief relied on the "separate but equal" doctrine announced by the Court in *Plessy* v. *Ferguson (supra).* That case stated that constitutionally required equality of treatment is attained when the races are provided substantially equal, although separate facilities. The Delaware court granted relief because the schools which black children attended in that area were substantially inferior. Therefore, the "separate but equal" doctrine could not validate Delaware's system.

*Holding:* (9x0) Students cannot be discriminated against in their admittance to the public schools on the basis of race.

*Basis:* The Fourteenth Amendment guarantees that students receive equal protection of the laws. The states' segregation of children in public schools solely on the basis of race deprives minority children of equal educational opportunities, even though the physical facilities and other tangible factors may be equal. Therefore, these school systems violate the equal protection clause of the Fourteenth Amendment.

# BOLLING v. SHARPE, 347 U.S. 497 (1954)

*Facts:*  Black children in Washington, D. C., were refused admission to public schools attended by white children solely on the basis of race. They challenged the constitutionality of the segregation of the public schools of the District of Columbia.

*Holding:*  (9x0) The federal government may not discriminate against the school children of Washington, D.C., on the basis of race.

*Bases:*  (1) The Fifth Amendment prohibits the federal government's denial of due process of law to the people. Since racial segregation serves no acceptable governmental purpose, the denial of liberty to black school children in order to achieve separation of the races is unconstitutional. (2) The Constitution, in the Fourteenth Amendment, prohibits the states from maintaining racially segregated public schools. It is unthinkable that the same Constitution would impose a lesser duty on the federal government.

# BROWN v. BOARD OF EDUCATION, 349 U.S. 294 (1955) *("Brown II")*

*Facts:*  *Brown I (supra)* declared the fundamental principle that racial discrimination in public education is unconstitutional. All provisions of federal, state, or local law requiring or permitting such discrimination must yield to this principle. Because of the complexities involved in moving from a dual, segregated system to a unitary system of public education, the Court here considered the suggestions of the parties involved, and of state and federal attorneys general. The Court then returned the cases to the local federal courts, from which they had come, for action in accord with the following guidelines and with the *Brown I* decision.

*Holding:*  (9x0) (1) Local school authorities have the primary responsibility for implementing the *Brown I* decision. The function of the federal courts is to decide whether a school board is complying in good faith and to reconcile the public interest in orderly and effective transition to constitutional school systems with the constitutional requirements themselves. (2) However, the principle of equal educational opportunity cannot yield simply because of public disagreement. A "prompt and reasonable start" toward full compliance must be made and compliance must proceed "with all deliberate speed."

*Basis:*     The Fourteenth Amendment, as interpreted in *Brown I,* guarantees students equal protection of the laws and requires that racially segregated public schools be declared unconstitutional.

## COOPER v. AARON, 358 U.S. 1 (1958)

*Facts:*     In compliance with the *Brown* decisions *(supra),* the Little Rock, Arkansas, School Board developed a plan for the gradual desegregation of the public schools. The plan called for the admission of nine blacks to a previously all-white high school. The state legislature passed laws intended to thwart implementation of the plan and the Governor dispatched troops to keep the black students from entering the high school. The public violently opposed the desegregation of the high school and the blacks were able to attend the school only under the protection of federal troops and at serious risk to their safety. In this case, the school board sought to postpone implementation of the desegregation plan because of the severity of the negative reaction to it.

*Holding:*     (8/1x0) Public hostility, especially when encouraged by the acts of the state legislature and other state officials, cannot justify the postponement of implementation of school desegregation plans.

*Basis:*     The Fourteenth Amendment, as interpreted by the *Brown* decisions, is the supreme law of the land and Article VI of the U.S. Constitution makes it binding on the states. The Fourteenth Amendment prohibits state action which denies people equal protection of the law. Thus, state support of segregated public schools is prohibited by the Fourteenth Amendment.

## GOSS v. BOARD OF EDUCATION, 373 U.S. 683 (1963)

*Facts:*     Two Tennessee schools boards proposed desegregation plans which provided for the rezoning of school districts without reference to race. Each plan also contained a transfer provision under which any student would be permitted, solely on the basis of his/her own race and the racial composition of the school to which he/she was assigned by virtue of rezoning, to transfer from such a school where he/she would be in the racial minority back to his/her former segregated school. The transfer provisions clearly worked to move students in one direction, across racially neutral zoning lines and back into segregated schools. Black students challenged the validity of these desegregation plans.

*Holding:*    (9x0) No official transfer plan which works to produce racially segregated schools and which is based on racial factors can be valid.

*Basis:*    The Fourteenth Amendment prohibits state action which denies equal protection of the law. State action creating or maintaining segregated public schools is prohibited under this Amendment.

## GRIFFIN v. COUNTY SCHOOL BOARD, 377 U.S. 218 (1964)

*Facts:*    In 1954, *Brown I (supra)* held that Virginia school segregation laws were unconstitutional and ordered that black students in Prince Edward County be admitted to the public schools on a racially nondiscriminatory basis "with all deliberate speed." Faced with an order to desegregate, the county school board refused, in 1959, to appropriate funds for the operation of public schools. However, tax credits were given for contributions to private white schools. The students in these private schools became eligible for county and state tuition grants in 1960. Public schools continued to operate elsewhere in Virginia. The local federal court ordered the reopening of the public schools. The validity of this court order was in question here.

*Holding:*    (7/2x0) The school board's action in closing county public schools while at the same time giving state financial assistance to white, private school students is unconstitutional. The time for mere "deliberate speed" has run out and that phrase can no longer justify the denial of equal educational opportunity to black students. The local court may order the reopening of the public schools.

*Basis:*    The equal protection clause of the Fourteenth Amendment requires that the states provide equal educational opportunity to black and to white students. The closing of public schools while state financial aid is given to white, private school students in the same county denies black children equal educational opportunity and is therefore unconstitutional.

## BRADLEY v. SCHOOL BOARD OF CITY OF RICHMOND, 382 U.S. 103 (1965) *("Bradley I")*

*Facts:*    Plans for desegregating two school systems were approved by the local district court although they did not contain provisions for the nonracial assignment of school teachers within the districts.

*Holding:*    (9x0 per curiam) (1) The assignment of faculty on a nonracial basis is an important factor and must be considered in a desegregation plan. (2) Evidentiary bearings should be provided.

*Bases:*    (1) The Fourteenth Amendment, as interpreted in the *Brown* decisions *(supra)*, requires desegregation of the public schools previously segregated by law or by state action. Racially neutral assignment of teachers, when proposed by those seeking to desegregate schools, is a factor which merits serious consideration. (2) The Court was unable to decide on the merits of the case because at the district court level there had not been a full evidentiary hearing on the issue.

## ROGERS v. PAUL, 382 U.S. 198 (1965)

*Facts:*    The desegregation plan adopted by the school system was a "grade a year" plan. This meant that some high school students were still attending segregated classes. The blacks attended a high school which did not have the range of courses offered at the white high school. In this case, black students challenged this situation and also the allocation of faculty at all grade levels on a racial basis.

*Holding:*    (5/4x0 per curiam) (1) Where equal course offerings are not available to black students in grades that have not yet been desegregated under a "grade a year" plan, the black students must be admitted immediately to the white school which has a superior curriculum. (2) The racial allocation of teachers denies students an equal educational opportunity and is unconstitutional. Students seeking desegregation of the school system are entitled to a hearing at which the basis of teacher allocation can be established.

*Basis:*    The Fourteenth Amendment as interpreted in the *Brown* decisions *(supra)* requires, at this date, immediate establishment of unitary school systems in those districts previously

84

segregated by law or by state action. The time for "all deliberate speed" has passed.

## GREEN v. COUNTY SCHOOL BOARD, 391 U.S. 430 (1968)

*Facts:*    The New Kent County school system in Virginia was serving about 1,300 students, approximately half of which were black. There was no residential segregation in the county and persons of both races resided throughout. The school system had only two schools, one for whites and one for blacks. Each school served the whole county and 21 buses traveled overlapping routes in order to transport students to segregated classes. In 1965, the school board, in order to remain eligible for federal financial aid, adopted a "freedom of choice" plan for desegregating the schools. The plan permitted students, except those entering the first and eighth grades, to choose annually between schools. Those not choosing were assigned to the school they had previously attended. First and eighth graders had to affirmatively choose a school. During the plan's three years of operation no white student had chosen to attend the all-black school, and although 115 blacks had enrolled in the formerly all-white school, 85% of the black students in the system still attended the all-black school. The adequacy of this desegregation plan was challenged in this case.

*Holding:*    (9x0) A "freedom of choice" plan, when established in a district with a long history of segregated schooling, offers little real promise that the required, unitary, nonsegregated school system will be established. A desegregation plan that is ineffective must be discontinued and an effective plan must be established.

*Basis:*    The Fourteenth Amendment, as interpreted in the *Brown* decisions *(supra)* requires unitary, desegregated school systems. Thirteen years after the *Brown* decisions, ineffective plans cause intolerable delay. Effective plans must be adopted immediately so that the Fourteenth Amendment requirement of equal protection under the law for black students can be met.

## MONROE v. BOARD OF COMMISSIONERS, 391 U.S. 450 (1968)

*Facts:*    In an effort to desegregate its elementary and junior high school systems, the City of Tucson instituted a "free-transfer" plan, which permitted a child, after registering in his/her assigned

85

school in his/her attendance zone, to transfer freely to another school of his/her choice if space were available. After three years of operation of the plan, the one black junior high school in the system was still completely black, one of the two white junior high schools was still almost all white, and three of the eight elementary schools were still attended only by blacks. The black children challenged the adequacy of this plan and of the school board's efforts to meet its responsibility to effect a transition to a unitary school system.

*Holding:*    (9x0) A free-transfer plan which does not result in effective desegregation is inadequate and does not constitute compliance with the order creating in the school board an affirmative duty to convert to a unitary school system.

*Basis:*    No official transfer plan or provision, of which racial segregation is the inevitable consequence, may stand under the Fourteenth Amendment. If it cannot be shown that a transfer plan will further, rather than delay, conversion to a unitary, nonracial, nondiscriminatory school system, it is unacceptable.

## UNITED STATES v. MONTGOMERY COUNTY BOARD OF EDUCATION, 395 U.S. 225 (1969)

*Facts:*    From 1964 to 1969, the local district court worked to push the desegregation of the county's schools. The general pattern was one of tokenism and delay on the part of the school board and patience and persistence on the part of the court. The nonracial allocation of faculty was a facet of the program which was especially lagging. The court finally ordered the nonracial allocation of faculty and required school board compliance with definite mathematical ratios. The reliance on mathematical ratios was challenged by the school board in this case.

*Holding:*    (9x0) In view of the pattern of lagging compliance by the school board and the judge's record of fairness and patience, the need for specific goals is evident and the numerical ratios are proper guidelines for desegregation.

*Basis:*    The Fourteenth Amendment prohibits state action denying people equal protection of the law, and, as interpreted by the *Brown* decision *(Supra)*, requires the establishment of nonracial school systems in those districts previously segregated by law or by state action. The nonracial assignment of faculty is part of this requirement.

## ALEXANDER v. HOLMES COUNTY BOARD OF EDUCATION, 396 U.S. 19 (1969)

*Facts:*    The Fifth Circuit Court of Appeals granted a motion for additional time and delayed implementation of an earlier order mandating desegregation in some Mississippi school districts educating thousands of children. This delay was challenged in this case.

*Holding:*    (9x0 per curiam) Delay can no longer be tolerated and the Court of Appeals must order immediate desegregation of the school districts. Modifications of and objections to the order may be considered while the order is implemented, but the implementation cannot be delayed any longer.

*Basis:*    The equality of educational opportunity required by the Fourteenth Amendment and by the *Brown* decision *(supra)* can no longer be delayed. The rights of black students must be supported by the courts. Delays should not be granted and amendments to desegregation plans must be reviewed by the courts and permitted only if they will work to further the goal of desegregation.

## DOWELL v. BOARD OF EDUCATION, 396 U.S. 269 (1969)

*Facts:*    The school board's desegregation proposal for immediate alteration of school attendance zones was approved by the trial court, and the school board was ordered to submit comprehensive plans for the desegregation of the entire school system. Upon being challenged, the order approving the attendance zone changes was vacated by the court of appeals, which stated that action should await the adoption of the comprehensive plan. The court of appeals' decision was challenged by black students.

*Holding:*    (9x0) The immediate change of attendance zones to promote desegregation should be permitted, pending formulation of a comprehensive desegregation plan.

*Basis:*    The Fourteenth Amendment requires, at this late date, immediate desegregation of school systems segregated by state action. Desegregation orders are to be implemented pending appeal, as further delay can no longer be tolerated.

## CARTER v. WEST FELICIANA PARISH SCHOOL BOARD, 396 U.S. 290 (1970)

*Facts:*      Soon after the Court in *Alexander* v. *Holmes County Board of Education (supra)* vacated a lower court order granting a three-month delay in desegregation and mandated immediate action, the Fifth Circuit Court of Appeals decided *Singleton* v. *Jackson Municipal Separate School District,* 419 F. 2d 1211 (5th Cir. 1959). This case was a consolidation of sixteen major school cases and involved hundreds of thousands of school children. The Fifth Circuit was reluctant to require relocation of these children in the middle of an ongoing school year and therefore required desegregation of faculties, facilities, activities, staff and transportation no later than February 1, 1970, but delayed integration of the student bodies until the beginning of the next school year. Here, an order was sought to reverse the order to delay student integration.

*Holding:*    (1/2/4/2x0 per curiam) Immediate desegregation of the student bodies is required. A maximum period of eight weeks is allowed for implementation of this order.

*Basis:*      The Fourteenth Amendment's equal protection clause requires desegregation of public school systems where such segregation is caused or supported by the state action. The time for "all deliberate speed" is past. Compliance with constitutional requirements must be immediate and complete.

## GRIGGS v. DUKE POWER CO., 401 U.S. 424 (1971)

*Facts:*      Prior to July 2, 1965, when the 1964 Civil Rights Act took effect, the Duke Power Company had openly discriminated on the basis of race in the hiring and assignment of employees in its Dan River Plant. In 1955, the Company began to require that employees have a high school diploma for initial assignment to any but the lowest paid, traditionally black department and for transfer to the higher paying white departments. In 1965, the Company began to require that transferees to higher paid, white departments obtain satisfactory scores on professionally-prepared general aptitude tests as well. It was shown that whites who met neither of these criteria had been adequately performing jobs in the higher paid departments for years. Black employees challenged these diploma and testing requirements which tend to render a disproportionate number of blacks ineligible for employment and transfer.

*Holding:*   (8x0) Diploma or degree requirements and generalized aptitude tests cannot be used when they work to disqualify a disproportionate number of minority group members unless the employer can show a direct correlation between the skills tested and adequate on-the-job performance. The requirements here in question have not been shown to be directly related to job performance and are therefore invalid.

*Basis:*   Title VII section 703 (h) of the Civil Rights Act of 1964 prohibits employers from using tests and diploma requirements which work to disqualify a disproportionate number of minority group members unless such tests are shown to be directly indicative of the ability to perform adequately on the job.

## WILLIAMS v. MCNAIR, 316 F. Supp. 134 (D.S.C. 1970), *aff'd,* 401 U.S. 951 (1971)

*Facts:*   The South Carolina system of higher education consists of eight colleges and universities. Most of these institutions are co-educational but one has historically been limited to males and another, the college at issue in this case, has historically been limited to females. The college for females specializes in a curriculum teaching secretarial and drawing skills as well as offering a general liberal arts education. The school for males offers a general education and is, in addition, a military school. In this case, male students who sought to be degree candidates at the girls' school argued that a sex-based limitation on enrollment is per se unconstitutional. They did not claim that they were denied the opportunity to take any particular course of study, nor did they claim that the single-sex policy at the girls' school relegated the men to attendance at a less prestigious institution.

*Decision:*   Summarily affirmed (8x1)

*Holding:*   (of the three-judge lower court): Where a limited number of state-supported schools which are part of a general co-educational system are restricted to one sex in order to further a program of education of generally greater interest to one sex, there is no constitutional violation and an open admissions policy will not be ordered.

*Basis:* Since the male students have access to similar course offerings at equally prestigious state institutions and since single-sex education is supported by a large number of responsible educators, the state operation of single-sex schools in order to further certain programs of study is rational and is not an arbitrary denial of the Fourteenth Amendment's guarantee of equal protection of the laws.

## SWANN v. CHARLOTTE-MECKLENBURG BOARD OF EDUCATION, 402 U.S. 1 (1971)

*Facts:* The Charlotte-Mecklenburg school system, with a student body which was 71% white and 29% black remained largely segregated in 1969, despite a 1965 desegregation plan based upon geographic zoning with a free-transfer provision. After the school board failed to produce a new plan, one was imposed by the district court. This plan grouped several outlying elementary schools with each black inner city school and required extensive busing. The plan also required that as many schools as practicable reflect the 71/29 white/black ratio then existing in the district as a whole. Here, the new plan was challenged as too burdensome.

*Holding:* (9x0) When school authorities fail to devise effective remedies for state-imposed segregation, the district courts have broad discretion to fashion a remedy that will assure transition to a unitary school system. (1) District courts may constitutionally order that teachers be assigned to achieve a certain degree of faculty desegregation. (2) District courts may forbid patterns of school construction and abandonment which serve to perpetuate or reestablish a dual system. (3) Racial quotas, when used not as inflexible requirements but as a starting point for the shaping of a desegregation plan, may be imposed by the courts. Once desegregation is achieved, school boards will not be required to make yearly adjustments in the racial composition of student bodies. (4) District courts may alter school attendance zones, may group and pair noncontiguous zones, and may require busing to a school not closest to the students' homes in order to achieve desegregation. Only when the travel time is excessive will objections to busing for integration be sustained.

*Basis:* The equal protection clause of the Fourteenth Amendment as interpreted in *Brown I (supra)* forbids state segregation of public schools on the basis of race. When school authorities default in their obligation to provide acceptable remedies, the district courts have broad power to fashion a remedy that will assure a unitary school system.

## DAVIS v. BOARD OF SCHOOL COMMISSIONERS, 402, U.S. 33 (1971)

*Facts:* The metropolitan area of Mobile, Alabama, is divided by a major north-south highway. About 94% of the black students in the metropolitan area live east of the highway. The schools in the western section were relatively easy to desegregate. However, the plan formulated by the Department of Justice and approved by the court of appeals resulted in nine nearly all-black schools in the eastern section (serving 64% of all of the black elementary school students in the metropolitan area). In addition, over half of the black junior and senior high school students in metropolitan Mobile were attending all-or nearly all-black schools. The plan which resulted in this number of black schools dealt with the eastern and western sections separately and did not provide for the movement of students across the highway as a means for effective desegregation. In this case, the adequacy of the plan was challenged.

*Holding:* (9x0) Plans to create constitutionally mandated unitary school systems are not limited by the neighborhood school concept. The transition from a segregated to a unitary school system should include every effort to achieve actual desegregation. Bus transportation and split zoning must be given adequate consideration by courts in formulating effective plans and must be used when other measures are ineffective.

*Basis:* The equal protection clause of the Fourteenth Amendment creates a *present* right in black school children to public education free of state-created or state-supported segregation. A school system that has operated under state segregative policies has an immediate duty to make an effective transition to unitary schools. The time for delay has passed; effective action is required now.

## MCDANIEL v. BARRESI, 402 U.S. 39 (1971)

*Facts:*    The Board of Education of Clarke County, Georgia, (with a white-black ratio of pupils in the elementary school system of approximately two-to-one) devised a student assignment plan for desegregating elementary schools. The plan relied primarily upon geographic attendance zones drawn to achieve greater racial balance. Additionally, the pupils in five heavily black attendance zones either walked or were transported by bus to schools located in other attendance zones. The resulting black elementary enrollment ranged from 20% to 40% in all by two schools, where it was 50%. Parents of the white students sued to enjoin the plan's operation, alleging that it violated the equal protection clause "by treating students differently because of their race and that transporting pupils in order to achieve racial balance is prohibited by Title IV of the Civil Rights Act."

*Holding:*    (9x0) School boards that operate dual school systems are charged with the affirmative duty to take whatever steps might be necessary, including transporting students based on race, to convert to a unitary system in which racial discrimination would be eliminated.

*Bases:*    (1) The transition from a dual to a unitary school system will almost invariably require that students be assigned differently on the basis of race, and the equal protection clause of the Fourteenth Amendment requires rather than prohibits this. (2) The plan is not barred by Title IV of the Civil Rights Act since the act is directed only at federal officials and does not restrict state officials in assigning students within their systems.

## GUEY HUNG LEE v. JOHNSON, 404 U.S. 1215 (1971)

*Facts:*    Until 1947, the California Education Code provided for the establishment of separate schools for students of Chinese ancestry. In the years following repeal of that code section, the San Francisco school board repeatedly drew school attendance zones which tended to perpetuate Chinese majority schools. In this case, people of Chinese ancestry sought to stay implementation of a court-approved desegregation plan which would alter the school attendance of students of Chinese ancestry.

*Holding:*    (one-judge opinion in chambers): Where school segregation has been fostered by state law and state action, prompt steps to

92

effectively desegregate the school system must be taken and delay can only be permitted in most unusual circumstances. Since no such circumstances exist in this case, no delay can be permitted.

*Basis:*  The equal protection clause of the Fourteenth Amendment requires that state segregation of education be remedied promptly. The Fourteenth Amendment applies not only to blacks but to all recognized minority groups and requires desegregation of all school systems segregated pursuant to state law and action.

## SPENCER v. KUGLER, 326 F. Supp. 1235 (D.N.J. 1971), *aff'd.,* 404 U.S. 1027 (1972)

*Facts:*  New Jersey state law creates municipal school districts whose boundaries coincide with municipal boundaries. Housing patterns and population shifts caused some municipalities and, therefore, some school districts to have a preponderance of black students. In this case, black students challenging this system of school districting sought redistricting for the purpose of desegregation and remedial programs for black districts presently segregated.

*Decision:*  Summarily affirmed (8x1)

*Holding:*  (of the three-judge lower court): A state law establishing a reasonable system of school districting that is not segregative in intent is constitutional even though subsequent population shifts result in *de facto* school segregation under the system so established.

*Basis:*  (of the lower court decision): The equal protection clause of the Fourteenth Amendment prohibits state action which deliberately establishes or aids racially segregated schools. However, in the absence of intentional governmental segregative action, federal courts cannot alter the assignment of students in order to remedy racial imbalance caused by population shifts.

## JEFFERSON PARISH SCHOOL BOARD v. DANDRIDGE, 404 U.S. 1219 (1971)

*Facts:*  In 1971, after seven years of litigation, the school board, which had repeatedly balked at the desegregation of the schools, was ordered to desegregate its schools. Although there were no more than normal difficulties incident to the transition from segregated to unitary schools, the school board sought a stay of the desegregation order.

Holding:     (one-judge opinion in chambers): Where no more than the usual and temporary difficulties incident to school desegregation are anticipated and where the school board has persistently balked at school desegregation, further delay will not be permitted.

Basis:     The Fourteenth Amendment, as interpreted by *Brown II (supra)*, requires that school systems segregated by state action be desegregated promptly.

## WRIGHT v. COUNCIL OF CITY OF EMPORIA, 407 U.S. 451 (1972)

Facts:     Until the 1969-70 school year, the public schools in Greenville County, Virginia, were run on a segregated basis. All of the white students in the county attended schools located in the city of Emporia. Black students attended schools located largely outside of Emporia. There was one school for blacks in Emporia. In 1967, Emporia changed its status from a "town" to a "city" that could, under state law, maintain a separate school system. However, until a court-ordered adoption of a plan by which all children enrolled in a particular grade level would attend the same school, Emporia chose to remain part of the county school system. After the desegregation order, Emporia withdrew from the county system and proposed a plan for an Emporia-only desegregated school district. Emporia's proposal would have resulted in the perpetuation of the division between better-equipped white schools in Emporia and black county schools. Its validity was challenged here.

Holding:     (5/4x0) Segregation has been county-wide. The withdrawal of Emporia, the site of the better equipped, traditionally white schools, from the county school system impedes the dismantling of the unconstitutional, segregated school system and is therefore not to be permitted.

Basis:     Because the effect of Emporia's withdrawal from the county system would be to impede the establishment of a desegregated school system and to perpetuate a dual school pattern, the

Fourteenth Amendment forbids the establishment of a separate Emporia school district at this time, while the transition from a segregated system to a unitary system is under way.

## UNITED STATES v. SCOTLAND NECK CITY BOARD OF EDUCATION, 407 U.S. 484 (1972)

*Facts:*   The schools of Halifax County, North Carolina, were completely segregated by race until 1965. In that year, the school board adopted a "freedom-of-choice" plan that resulted in little actual desegregation. In 1968, the Department of Justice and the school board agreed to a plan to create a unitary system for Halifax County in the 1969-70 school year. In 1969, a bill was passed by the state legislature enabling the city of Scotland Neck which was part of the county school district to create, by majority vote, its own separate school district. The newly created district would be 57% white and 43% black. The schools in the rest of Halifax County would be about 90% black. Thus the effect of this plan would be to nullify the 1968 desegregation plan and to maintain a system in which Scotland Neck schools were largely white and the outlying schools were largely black. Its validity was challenged in this case.

*Holding:*   (5/4x0) The dismantling of a segregated school system cannot be impeded by the legislative creation of two new districts, one white and one black. The state action dividing Halifax County into two school districts interferes with the desegregation which is required by law and is therefore unconstitutional.

*Basis:*   The Fourteenth Amendment, as interpreted in the *Brown* decision *(supra),* forbids state action creating, supporting, or perpetuating segregated public schools. That the state action involved here was by the legislature rather than by the school board does not change its segregative effect or make it valid.

## DRUMMOND v. ACREE, 409 U.S. 1228 (1972)

*Facts:*   The district court ordered the transportation of students to accomplish desegregation of the elementary school system of Augusta, Georgia. In this case, parents sought a stay of the order, premised solely on the federal statute, Title VIII, section 803 which reads:

95

In the case of any order on the part of any United States district court which requires the transfer or transportation of any student . . . for the purposes of achieving a balance among students with respect to race . . . , the effectiveness of such order shall be postponed until all appeals . . . have been exhausted.

*Holding:* (one-judge opinion in chambers): Title VIII, section 803 does not act to block orders requiring the transportation of students for the purpose of desegregating a school system. It postpones implementation only of those orders requiring the transportation of any student for the purpose of achieving a balance among the students with respect to race.

*Basis:* The district court order was entered to accomplish desegregation of a school system not for the purpose of achieving a racial balance as contemplated by section 803. The constitutional command to desegregate schools does not mean that every school in every community must always reflect the racial composition of the school system as a whole.

## KEYES v. SCHOOL DISTRICT NO. 1, DENVER, COLORADO, 413 U.S. 189 (1973)

Although the Denver, Colorado, school system had never been operated under a state constitutional provision or law that mandated or permitted school segregation, many of the city's schools were segregated. In 1969, the school board adopted a voluntary plan for the desegregation of the predominantly black Park Hill section of the city. A school board election was then held which resulted in a majority of the members opposed to the plan. Subsequently a court order was obtained which mandated the desegregation of the Park Hill section and found that the segregation in Park Hill had been caused by prior school board action. In this case, those favoring integration sought desegregation orders for the remaining schools in the district and the counting of Hispanic, as well as of black children, as minority students.

*Holding:* (5/1½x1½) (1) Absent a showing that a school district is divided into clearly unrelated units, proof of a state action, e.g., school board action causing segregation in a substantial portion of that district, supports a finding that the entire district is segregated. The court may order a district-wide remedy if, in fact, the segregation in one part of the district results in segregation in the rest of the district.

Once segregation fostered by state action is shown in one part of the district and it is shown that other schools in the district are segregated, the state would have to prove a lack of "segregative intent" with respect to the other schools to avoid a district-wide desegregation order. (2) For purposes of defining a segregated school, blacks and Hispanics should be considered together as minority students since both groups suffer the same educational inequities when compared to the education offered Anglo students.

*Basis:*   The Fourteenth Amendment prohibits state action which results in segregated public schools and which denies minority students equal protection of the law by denying them equal educational opportunity.

## NORWOOD v. HARRISON, 413 U.S. 455 (1973)

*Facts:*   Since 1940, Mississippi had been buying textbooks and lending them free to students in both public and private schools without reference to whether or not any participating private school had racially discriminatory policies. The number of private, non-sectarian schools had increased from seventeen in 1963-64 (white students enrolled numbered 2,170) to 155 in 1970-71 (white students numbered about 42,000). The creation and enlargement of these private schools was in direct response to the desegregation of the public schools. Thousands of students who were attending private, all-white schools were receiving free textbooks. While 90% of the state's school children still attended public schools, some school districts had lost all of their white students to private, segregated schools. There was no proof that, absent the free texts, any children would withdraw from segregated, private schools and enroll in unitary, public schools. The provision of texts to segregated, private schools at state expense was challenged here.

*Holding:*   (7/2x0) The state may not grant tangible, specific financial aid, e.g., free books, tuition grants, to private, segregated schools.

*Basis:*   Racial discrimination in state-operated schools is barred by the equal protection clause of the Fourteenth Amendment. The state may not induce, encourage, or promote private persons to accomplish what it may not constitutionally accomplish itself. The state provision of free texts may not be essential to the continued operation of private, segregated schools but it does

97

constitute substantial state support of discrimination and is therefore prohibited by the Fourteenth Amendment.

## LAU v. NICHOLS, 414 U.S. 563 (1974)

*Facts:*    The San Francisco school system, which according to state statute has the teaching of proficiency in English to all students as a major goal, failed to offer remedial English language instruction or any other special compensatory program to about 1,800 Chinese-speaking pupils. This class of pupils claimed that the school board was in violation of the equal protection clause of the Fourteenth Amendment and of section 601 of the Civil Rights Act of 1964, which prohibits recipients of federal aid from discriminating against students on the basis of race, color, or national origin. H.E.W. has authority under section 602 of the 1964 Act to promulgate regulations in furtherance of section 601. A pertinent H.E.W. guidelines states: "where inability to speak and understand the English language excludes national-origin minority group children from effective participation in the educational program offered by a school district, the district must take affirmative steps to rectify the language deficiency in order to open its instructional program to these students."

*Holding:*    (5/2/2x0) A school district receiving federal aid must provide special instruction for non-English speaking students whose education is severely hampered by the language barrier, at least when there are substantial numbers of such students within the district.

*Bases:*    (1) The failure to provide 1,800 non-English speaking students with special instruction denies them a meaningful opportunity to participate in the public education program and thus violates section 601 of the Civil Rights Act of 1964 and the H.E.W. regulations and guidelines implementing the Act. (2) The Court does not decide whether the failure to provide such a program is violative of the equal protection clause of the Fourteenth Amendment.

## CLEVELAND BOARD OF EDUCATION v. LAFLEUR, COHEN v. CHESTERFIELD COUNTY SCHOOL BOARD, 414 U.S. 632 (1974)

*Facts:*    Public school teachers, who became pregnant and who were obliged to leave work under mandatory maternity leave rules

98

before they so desired, challenged the constitutionality of the rules. The Cleveland rule required every pregnant teacher to take a maternity leave without pay beginning five months before the expected birth. Application for such leave was required to be made no later than two weeks prior to the date of departure. A teacher on maternity leave was not allowed to return to work until the beginning of the next regular school semester following the date when her child reached three months of age. A doctor's certificate of health was required.

The Chesterfield, Virginia, rule required that a pregnant teacher leave work at least four months prior to the expected birth. Notice was required to be given six months prior to the expected birth. Return to work was guaranteed no later than the first day of the school year following the date when the teacher presented a doctor's certificate and could assure the board that care of the child would cause only minimal interference with her job.

*Holding:* (5/2x2) While notice requirements are acceptable, mandatory termination dates established in both rules and the mandatory three-month period of ineligibility for return to work established in the Cleveland rule are unconstitutional. Pregnancy should be treated like any other temporary disability for all job-related purposes.

*Basis:* The mandatory termination provisions and the mandatory waiting period before return to work in the Cleveland rule violates the due process clause of the Fourteenth Amendment. Freedom of personal choice in matters of family life is a liberty protected by the Fourteenth Amendment and state rules affecting this liberty must not needlessly, arbitrarily, or capriciously impinge upon it. Since the ability of any particular pregnant teacher to continue or return to work is an individual matter, the rules creating conclusive presumptions of inability to work are violative of due process. The notice provisions are rationally related to school board needs for planning and do not impair the teachers' rights or offend the constitution.

## MAYOR OF PHILADELPHIA v. EDUCATIONAL EQUALITY LEAGUE, 415 U.S. 605 (1974)

*Facts:* Under the city charter, the mayor appointed both the Educational Nominating Panel and the nine members of the school board, who are nominated by the above-mentioned

99

panel. The nominating panel contains thirteen members, four of whom are chosen from the citizenry at large and nine of whom must each be the highest ranking officer of a governmental, community, or educational organization. There was some evidence that the mayor was unaware of black civic groups. whose officers ought to have been eligible for consideration. There was a newspaper report of the mayor's statement that he would appoint no more blacks to the school board in 1969.

The Educational Equality League charged that Mayor Tate unconstitutionally discriminated against blacks in making his appointments to the 1971 panel and sought an order barring that panel from nominating prospective school board members. It also sought an order mandating that the mayor correct the racial imbalance of the present panel and appoint racially balanced panels in the future, but it did not seek imposition of strict numerical quotas on the mayor's appointment power. Mayor Tate was succeeded in office by Mayor Rizzo. No evidence as to Mayor Rizzo's policies had been introduced.

*Holding:* (5x4) Where there is no clear evidence of racial discrimination in the appointment of the school board nominating panel, no action will be taken by the courts to alter the method of selection of appointees. The fact of numerical racial imbalance is not proof of unconstitutional discrimination in this case.

*Basis:* Absent clear evidence of a violation of the Fourteenth Amendment, the Court declines to interfere with the appointment power of governmental officials.

## BRADLEY v. SCHOOL BOARD, 416 U.S. 696 (1974) *("Bradley II")*

*Facts:* Following a long court battle for a more effective school desegregation plan which reached the Supreme Court (see *Bradley supra)* the federal district court awarded the parents and guardians of black students their expenses and attorneys' fees incurred during the litigation, and found that the actions taken and the defenses made by the school board had caused unreasonable delay in desegregation of the schools and had caused the parents to spend large sums in order to protect the children's constitutional rights. The court of appeals voided the award of fees because there was no federal statute authorizing such payment either at the time that the legal services were rendered or while the desegregation case was pending. Before the court of appeals reached its decision as to the propriety of the fee award, a law was passed authorizing such payments to deserving prevailing parties.

Holding:    (7x0) The law authorizing fee awards became effective while this case as to the propriety of such awards was pending. The law, therefore, may be applied to this case and may authorize payment for legal services rendered prior to the law's enactment.

Basis:      An appellate court must apply the law in effect at the time of the decision unless to do so would be unjust. The nature of the parties and rights involved and the law's effect on those rights determine the justice of its application to cases arising before its effective date. The law is properly applied to compensate parents who bore a heavy financial burden in order to vindicate a public right, and its application works no injustice on the school board whose duty to provide a unitary school system is unchanged by the law.

## GILMORE v. MONTGOMERY, 417 U.S. 556 (1974)

Facts:      In 1959, the district court ordered the city of Montgomery, Alabama, to desegregate its public parks. Thereafter, the city coordinated a program with the racially segregated Y.M.C.A. and managed to continue to run segregated recreational programs. This case was begun in 1971. The complaint was that the city permitted racially segregated, private schools and other segregated, private groups to use city recreational facilities.

Holding:    (5/3½x½) (1) The city may not permit segregated private schools and school groups to have exclusive access* to public recreational facilities. (2) If non-exclusive use by private school groups directly impairs an existing school desegregation order or constitutes a vestige of the type of state-sponsored segregation of the city's recreational facilities that was prohibited by the district court in 1959, it should be enjoined. (3) Unless it is shown that the city is actively participating in the discrimination practiced by segregated, non-school groups, it should not be enjoined from permitting such groups to use park

---

*The term "exclusive access" does not include the situation where only part of a facility may be allocated to or used by a group. For example, the use of two of a total of ten tennis courts by a private school group would not constitute an exclusive use; the use of all ten courts would.

101

facilities on an equal basis with other members of the public.

*Bases:* (1) The city was under an order to desegregate its schools in accord with requirements of the Fourteenth Amendment. The allocation of exclusive use of park facilities to private, segregated schools works to support those schools and constitutes state interference with the desegregation order which is unconstitutional. (2) The First Amendment's freedom of association prohibits the state from refusing access to private non-school groups merely because they are segregated. However, the Fourteenth Amendment prohibits state support of segregation.

## MILLIKEN v. BRADLEY, 418 U.S. 717 (1974) *("Milliken I")*

*Facts:* This case arose after a district court ordered a desegregation plan for Detroit's schools which encompassed a number of outlying school districts as well as the city of Detroit proper. Detroit did not have a history of segregation ordered or permitted by law. However, there was a long history of public and private discrimination that had helped to produce residential segregation. Detroit school children and their parents claimed that the school board's imposition of school attendance zones over the existing segregated residential pattern had produced an unconstitutional dual school system in Detroit. They cited the school board's policy in school construction and its approval of optional attendance zones in fringe areas. That unconstitutional segregation existed in Detroit was not questioned here. What is in question is the constitutionality of the court-ordered desegregation plan extending to outlying districts with no history of segregative action on the part of their school boards or local governments.

*Holding* (5x4) Absent a showing that the outlying districts have failed to operate unitary school systems or have committed acts that fostered segregation in other school districts, a court-ordered school desegregation plan cannot cross school district lines to include them in the plan.

*Basis:* The Fourteenth Amendment prohibits state action which denies minority group school children equal protection of the law by maintaining a segregated school system. The argument that the outlying districts are subdivisions of the state, that the state contributed to segregation in Detroit, and that, therefore, the outlying districts are subject to a multi-district school desegregation plan, is rejected. In order for a multi-district remedy to be ordered by a court, the local governments of outlying districts must have committed segregative acts.

**EVANS v. BUCHANAN, 393 F. Supp. 428 (D. Del. 1975),** *aff'd.,* **423 U.S. 963 (1975)**

*Facts:*    Action was brought complaining that black children in Wilmington, Delaware, were being compelled to attend segregated schools. The three-judge trial court held that presence of *de jure* black schools which remained identifiably black was a clear indication that segregated schooling had never been eliminated in the city and that there still existed a dual school system, despite adoption of racially neutral attendance zones. The court required the State Board of Education to come forward with plans to remedy existing segregation. Consequently, the state passed an act authorizing the Board of Education to consolidate school districts according to the dictates of sound educational administration. The Wilmington school district was explicitly excluded in the act from reorganization of state boards. The lower court held the statute to be unconstitutional. The school board challenged this ruling.

*Decision:*    Summarily affirmed (3x1)

*Holding:*    (of the three-judge court): Where a statute explicitly or effectively makes goals of racial minorities more difficult to achieve, such statute is unconstitutional.

*Basis:*    (of the lower court decision): Neither the purported state constitutional requirement, nor the state interest in preserving historic school district boundaries, nor the state interest in maintaining school districts with enrollment below 12,000 was, individually or cumulatively, a compelling state interest. Such an interest must be shown in cases of a suspect classification under the equal protection clause.

103

# WASHINGTON v. DAVIS, 426 U.S. 229 (1976)*

*Facts:* As part of its selection procedure for police academy recruits, Washington, D.C., officials adminstered "Test 21," which was also used generally in the federal civil service to test verbal ability. It was shown that a passing score on the test was positively correlated with successful completion of the course of study at the police academy. However, a positive correlation between a passing score on the test and the quality of an applicant's on-the-job performance was not shown. The Police Department actively sought black recruits and raised the percentage of black recruits so that it was roughly equal to the percentage of 20- to 29-year-old blacks in the area from which personnel were drawn. While there was no showing of discriminatory intent or action in administration of the test, four times more blacks than whites had failed the test. In this case, black applicants claimed that the test had a racially disproportionate impact and is therefore unconstitutional.

*Holding:* (4/3x2) A test that is racially neutral on its face, that is administered without racially discriminatory action or intent, and that is reasonably related to a legitimate state purpose, e.g., that of insuring a minimum level of verbal ability in police recruits, is constitutional.

*Bases:* (1) The due process clause of the Fifth Amendment prohibits the federal government from acting with racially discriminatory purpose. However, a law or other official act is not necessarily unconstitutional solely because it has a racially disproportionate impact. Here, the test was racially neutral on its face and was administered to serve a legitimate purpose. There was no official intent to discriminate and there is, therefore, no constitutional basis for invalidating the testing procedure. (2) Title VII of the Civil Rights Act of 1964 requires that applicant screening tests with disproportionate racial impact be abandoned unless the employer can show a direct correlation between skills tested and job performance. However, Title VII was not a basis for this decision since it was, at the time of this case, not applicable to federal employees. It has since been extended to cover such employees.

---

*For a subsequent Supreme Court decision that was vacated in light of *Washington v. Davis*, see *Austin Independent School Dist. v. United States*, 45 U.S.L.W. 3413 (Dec. 7, 1976).

## RUNYON v. MCCRARY, 427 U.S. 160 (1976)

*Facts:*      Two black children applied for admission to private, nonsectarian schools which advertised in the yellow pages and through bulk mailings in order to attract students. Both children were denied admission solely on the basis of race. In this case, the children challenged the private schools' acts of racial discrimination.

*Holding:*    (5/2x2) Private, nonsectarian schools which offer enrollment to qualified applicants from the public at large may not limit their offering to whites only and refuse admission to others solely on the basis of race.

*Bases:*      (1) The Thirteenth Amendment to the Constitution prohibits slavery and the badges and incidents of that condition. The Thirteenth Amendment also provides that the federal government shall enforce these prohibitions by appropriate legislation. Title 42 U.S.C. section 1981, which provides, in part, that all persons shall have the same right in every state to make and enforce contracts, is appropriate legislation under the Thirteenth Amendment. It prohibits private acts of racial discrimination in the offering of contracts to the public, e.g., contracts for employment or education. (2) The Court does not state that promotion of the concept of racial segregation is barred by 42 U.S.C. section 1981 and only prohibits implementation of such a policy. (3) The Court does not decide whether sectarian, private schools which practice racial discrimination for religious reasons are prohibited from doing so by 42 U.S.C. section 1981.

## PASADENA CITY BOARD OF EDUCATION v. SPANGLER, 427 U.S. 424 (1976)

*Facts:*      As a result of a law suit brought by parents, students, and the United States Government, the City of Pasadena was ordered to desegregate its public schools. The court order required that, beginning with the 1970-71 school year, there would be no school "with a majority of any minority students." The board of education assigned students in a racially neutral manner and in 1970-71 the "no majority" requirement was met. In the years following 1970-71, the school system had an increasing number of schools that were not in compliance with the requirement. This change in student population was not caused by segregative school board action but by random population shifts in the district. The board of education sought to have the "no majority of minority students" requirement dropped.

*Holding:* (6x2) (1) Although the students who originally brought the desegregation suit have graduated from the school system, the court orders may still be litigated since the United States remains an interested party. (2) Once desegregation of student populations is achieved to eliminate school system discrimination brought about by official action, school officials may not be required to make yearly alterations of student assignment plans in order to maintain a strict numerical ratio of majority to minority students. Such ratios may be used only as guidelines or starting points for the initial transition from segregated to unitary schools.

*Bases:* (1) Since the students have already graduated and no longer have a legal interest in Pasadena's public schools and since their court action was not properly certified as a class action, the case would be moot under Article III of the Constitution and the desegregation orders would be void but for the continued interest of the United States as authorized in the Civil Rights Act of 1964. (2) The Fourteenth Amendment requires the desegregation of school systems segregated by the public officials. Once desegregation is achieved there is no constitutional requirement of any particular racial ratio in the public schools.

## ARLINGTON HEIGHTS v. METROPOLITAN HOUSING DEVELOPMENT CORPORATION, 97 S. Ct. 568 (1977)*

*Facts:* Metropolitan, a non-profit builder, contracted to purchase land with boundaries on Arlington Heights in order to build racially integrated low- and moderate-income housing. Metropolitan applied for the necessary rezoning from a single-family to a multiple-family classification. The Village of Arlington denied Metropolitan's request. Metropolitan and individual minority persons filed suit to compel acceptance of their application, alleging that the denial was racially discriminatory and violated the equal protection clause of the Fourteenth Amendment and the Fair Housing Act of 1968. The

*For a subsequent Supreme Court decision which was vacated in light of *Arlington Heights v. Metropolitan Housing Development Corporation,* see *Metropolitan School Dist. v. Buckley,* 45 U.S.L.W. 3508 (Jan. 25, 1977).

federal district court held that Arlington's denial was motivated not by racial discrimination but by a desire to protect property values. The court of appeals reversed, finding that the "ultimate effect" of Arlington's denial was racially discriminatory. Arlington appealed the court of appeals' reversal.

*Holding:* (5/1x2) An official action that results in a racially disproportionate impact is not unconstitutional unless proof of a racially discriminatory intent or purpose is shown.

*Basis:* Disproportionate impact is not irrelevant to the equal protection clause of the Fourteenth Amendment, but it is not the sole touchstone of an invidious racial discrimination. Because legislators and administrators are properly concerned with balancing numerous competitive considerations, courts refrain from reviewing the merits of their decisions, absent a showing of arbitrariness or irrationality. However, racial discrimination is not just another competing factor. When there is proof that a discriminatory purpose has been a motivating factor in the decision, this judicial deference is no longer justified.

## VORCHEIMER v. SCHOOL DISTRICT OF PHILADELPHIA, 532 F. 2d 880 (3d Cir. 1976), *aff'd,* 97 S. Ct. 1671 (1977)

*Facts:* The Philadelphia School District offers college preparatory programs in two different types of high schools: academic and comprehensive. Comprehensive schools provide a wide range of courses, including those required for college admission. The criterion for enrollment in these schools is residency within a designated area and most of the schools are coeducational. There are only two academic high schools. These have high admission standards (only 7 percent of the city's students qualify) and serve the whole city. One school accepts only male students and the other accepts only females. The two schools are comparable in quality and offer essentially equal educational experiences. Enrollment in either school is voluntary and a student is free to choose a coeducational comprehensive school as an alternative. In this case, an academically qualified female student, who would have preferred to attend the academic high school for males and who was denied admittance there solely on the basis of her sex, challenged the constitutionality of her rejection.

*Decision:*    Summarily affirmed (4x4)*

*Holding:*    (of the three-judge lower court): If attendance at single sex high schools is voluntary, if coeducational alternatives are available, and if the educational opportunities offered at the schools for males and for females are comparable, then the maintenance of such schools is constitutional.

*Bases:*    (of the lower court decision): (1) The equal protection clause of the Fourteenth Amendment requires the states to provide all students with an equal educational opportunity. Students of both sexes must be afforded equal educational opportunity in all intellectual fields. However, the value of sex-segregated education has long been recognized and the existence of two voluntary, single-sex schools offering comparable services in a school system which is otherwise coeducational does not offend the Amendment. (2) The Equal Educational Opportunity Act of 1974 does not proscribe the maintenance of single-sex schools. Its language requires "equal educational opportunity" without regard to race, color, or sex; but the Congress, choosing to study the issue further, did not in this Act ban separate but equal sex-segregated schools.

## MILLIKEN v. BRADLEY, 45 U.S.L.W. 4873 (June 27, 1977) ("Milliken II")

*Facts:*    In *Milliken I (supra)* the Supreme Court decided that the district court's interdistrict remedy for *de jure* segregation in the Detroit school system was not constitutionally mandated and the case was sent back to that court for the formulation of a Detroit-only remedy. The district court's new order consisted of a Detroit-only pupil assignment plan and of four remedial educational programs designed to combat the effects of prior *de jure* segregation. These programs, which had been proposed by the Detroit School board, were in the areas of remedial reading, in-service teacher training, student testing, and counseling. The district court ordered that one half the cost of these programs would be borne by the school district and that the other one half would be borne by the state. In this case, the state challenged the district court's authority to order remedial programs and its power to allocate one half the financial burden for such programs to the state.

---

*Negligible, if any, precedential value.

| | |
|---|---|
| *Holding:* | (8/2x0) (1) As part of a desegregation decree a district court can order remedial educational and supportive programs for children who have been subjected to *de jure* segregation in the past. This is especially true when such programs are supported by evidence and proposed by the local school board. (2) The court may constitutionally require that the state pay one half of the cost of such remedial programs. |
| *Bases:* | (1) The Fourteenth Amendment prohibits *de jure* segregation in public schools and requires that *de jure* segregated schools be converted to unitary ones. The federal courts giving consideration to the scope of the constitutional violation, the interests of local governments in managing school affairs, and the remedial nature of a desegregation order may require programs as well as pupil assignment plans in order to implement the transition to a unitary school system. (2) The Eleventh Amendment, which protects the states from financial liability for past acts of state officials, does not bar courts from ordering a state to participate in or financially support compliance with the constitutionally mandated desegregation of public schools. The Tenth Amendment protects the states from federal interference with their governmental form and functioning, but does not preclude a federal court ordering that state funds be expended in the implementation of Fourteenth Amendment guarantees. |

## HAZLEWOOD SCHOOL DISTRICT v. UNITED STATES, 45 U.S.L.W. 4882 (1977)

| | |
|---|---|
| *Facts:* | In the Hazlewood School District, which is located in St. Louis County, the percentage of black teachers was 1.4% in 1972-73 and 1.8% in 1973-74. In St. Louis County as a whole, the percentage of black teachers was 15.4% during those years. The city of St. Louis was, during that time, attempting to maintain a 50% black teaching staff. Excluding the city, the percentage of black teachers in the county was 5.7 percent. Title VII of the Civil Rights Act of 1964 which prohibits racial discrimination in hiring and employment, became applicable to school district in March of 1972. Hazlewood school district hired 3.7% black teachers in 1972-74. In this case, Hazlewood school district challenged a lower court ruling based on a comparison of the racial composition of St. Louis County's teaching force with that of the school district's. The ruling states that the district has engaged in discriminatory practices in violation of Title VII. |

| | |
|---|---|
| *Holding:* | (8/2x1) Citing the *Teamsters* case *(supra),* the Court ruled that "where gross statistical disparities can be shown, they alone may in a proper case constitute *prima facie* proof of a pattern or practice of discrimination." In determining whether an employer's hiring practices are in violation of Title VII of the 1964 Civil Rights Act, a court should compare the number of qualified minority group members available for employment in the relevant labor pool with the number of minority group members hired by the employer in question. (1) This comparison should be concerned only with the number of minority group members hired since the effective date of the Act, as employers are not liable for pre-Act discrimination. (2) When area employers make special efforts to hire minority group members the percentages of such employees in their work force may not properly reflect the number of qualified minority group members as a whole in the labor pool, and this should be taken into consideration when a determination as to employment discrimination is being made. |
| *Basis:* | Title VII of the Civil Rights Act of 1964 prohibits discrimination in hiring and employment but will not require that remedial measures be taken when a low percentage of minority group employees in the work force is caused only by pre-Act patterns of discrimination. |

**DAYTON BOARD OF EDUCATION v. BRINKMAN, 45 U.S.L.W. 4910 (June 27, 1977)**

| | |
|---|---|
| *Facts:* | The district court found that *de jure* segregation existed in the Dayton, Ohio, school district. It based its findings on the following three factors: (1) substantial racial imbalance in student bodies throughout the system, (2) the school board's use of optional attendance zones for high schools which had a segregative effect, (The district court found that the use of such zones was racially neutral at the elementary school level and the court also found that no students in the optional zone were denied their choice of school because of race.) (3) the school board's rescinding of a prior board's resolutions acknowledging the board's role in racial segregation and calling for remedial measures. The district court at the insistence of the court of appeals ordered a school system-wide remedy, the propriety of which was challenged here. |
| *Holding:* | (7/2x0) Where segregative acts of a school board are not shown |

to have system-wide effect, a system-wide remedy cannot properly be imposed. (1) The existence of racially imbalanced schools does not warrant court-ordered remedial action in the absence of a showing of causation by segregative acts of the state or school board. (2) Such a segregative act, the use of the optional zone for high school students, had only been found at the secondary school level. (3) The rescinding of the prior board's resolution calling for desegregation action is not a segregative act unless evidence establishes the existence of prior *de jure* segregation. The case is remanded so that the district court may establish whether other segregative acts of the school board can be established so as to warrant a system-wide remedy, or whether a more limited order must be formulated. Pending new determination, the district court's present plan is to take effect.

*Basis:*    The Fourteenth Amendment forbids the states to engage in acts which establish or further segregate public schools. The power of the courts to order remedial measures to combat segregation is dependent on the scope of the Fourteenth Amendment's prohibition. Therefore, courts can only order desegregation of schools in which segregation is the product of governmental action.

111

# VI.  PROCEDURAL PARAMETERS

*Reviewers:*   Aviam Soifer
               Professor
               School of Law
               University of Connecticut

               Perry A. Zirkel
               Dean and Professor
               School of Education
               Lehigh University

The cases in this chapter illustrate some of the procedural hurdles which must be overcome in order to obtain a ruling on the substantive issue(s) presented to the Court. The two major procedural hurdles relate to the justiciability of the issues and the standing of the parties. These concepts are interrelated and flexible, presenting a source of discretion and evolution for the Court.

There is a constitutional requirement that cases or controversies be "concrete," which in legal terminology is referred to as justiciability. Thus, the substantive claim may be moot and not proper for decisions due to the lengthy trial and appeal process before the case reaches the Supreme Court. For example, in the *Doremus* and *DeFunis* cases, the substantive issues had become moot because of the graduation of the plaintiff-students during the course of the litigation. A jurisdictional requirement of federal courts related to concreteness is the limitation to "substantial federal questions," i.e., those involving federal statutes, treaties, and the Constitution. Thus, the Court declined to decide *Ellis* and *San Mateo* for lack of this jurisdictional element. Another restriction is the impropriety of deciding collusive suits, when the parties are not truly adverse. Finally, it has been held improper for a federal court to issue advisory opinions, which either are not framed as law suits or involve issues not properly subject to judicial resolution.

Standing of the parties similarly stems from the Court's institutional avoidance of abstract or hypothetical matters. The complainant must show an actual stake in the outcome of the case. The interest or injury may be financial, as in *Flast,* or personal, as in *Mercer.* Plaintiffs, generally, may not plead the interests of others except as they qualify for class actions, as outlined in the *Jacobs* case.

The cases which follow, although they often represent vacated and dismissed decisions, provide perspective as to the institutional parameters of courts generally and the singular position of the Supreme Court specifically. For those who seek a hearing from the Court or wish to understand its decisions, such procedural parameters provide an important, but often neglected, context. Thus, these cases are a fitting end to the digest.

## DOREMUS v. BOARD OF EDUCATION, 5 N.J. 435 (1950), *dismissed,* 342 U.S. 429 (1952)

*Facts:*    The parent of a child, who in the interim graduated from the school system, and a resident, who is a taxpayer of the school district, challenged the validity of a New Jersey statute which provided for the reading of five verses from the Old Testament at the beginning of each school day.

*Holding:*    (6x3) The Court cannot decide the constitutional issue raised by these two complainants since (1) the claim of a child who has graduated from the school system is moot, i.e., no longer a live controversy; and since (2) the taxpayer cannot show how the time spent in Bible recitation directly costs sufficient tax dollars to give him a particular financial interest in having the statute invalidated.

*Basis:*    The Court is limited by Article III of the Constitution to consideration of concrete cases or controversies. Since neither of the complaining parties has a sufficiently active interest in the issue, the Court lacks jurisdiction over the case.

## ELLIS v. DIXON, 120 N.Y.S. 2d. 854 (1953), *dismissed,* 349 U.S. 458 (1955)

*Facts:*    Members of the Yonkers Committee for Peace brought an action claiming that the school board had unconstitutionally denied them the use of a school building for a forum on peace and war. The members did not challenge the school board's right to regulate reasonably nonschool use of school buildings, nor did they challenge the board's regulations as unconstitutionally vague. They asserted that other organizations had been permitted to use school buildings; however, they did not present evidence that they were similar to those other organizations and had therefore been unfairly treated under school board classifications and regulations. Their complaint was dismissed by the state trial court and their request to be heard on the state appellate level was denied. They challenged the state court action.

*Holding:* (5x4) The Committee did not present a case which must be decided on federal grounds, since it now appeared that the state court rulings rested on adequate state grounds. The Court dismisses the writ of *certiorari,* as improvidently presented.

*Bases:* (1) The Court cannot decide this case on federal constitutional grounds since insufficient facts were presented in the record of the lower court proceeding to form the basis for such a claim. (2) Since the Court assumes that the state court's denial of the Committee's request to appeal was based on adequate nonfederal grounds, the Court has no jurisdiction to consider the case anew.

## FLAST v. COHEN, 392 U.S. 83 (1968)

*Facts:* Titles I and II of the Elementary and Secondary Education Act of 1965 mandated the expenditure of federal funds for educational materials and inschool services to both public and religious school children. Federal income taxpayers sought a declaration that the disbursement of public funds to religious schools was unconstitutional. A federal district court dismissed their complaint and ruled that, as taxpayers, they lacked sufficient interest in the matter to maintain the federal action in court.

*Holding:* (5/3x1) A taxpayer may challenge a statute in federal court if he/she can show that it is: (1) an exercise of Congress's power to tax and to spend (rather than a primarily regulatory act requiring only an incidental expenditure of funds for administration); and (2) in violation of a specific constitutional guarantee, e.g., the First Amendment's prohibition of governmental establishment of religion and therefore beyond the Congress's spending power.

*Bases:* (1) Article III of the U.S. Constitution requires those persons bringing federal suits to have "standing," that is, a personal stake in the outcome of the litigation. Taxpayers have a personal stake in being free of taxing and spending that is in contravention of specific constitutional limitations of Congress's taxing and spending power. (2) The Court does not decide in this case whether the statute in question violates the

114

establishment clause of the First Amendment. The Court only decides that federal taxpayers have standing to seek judicial determination of this question.

## JOHNSON v. NEW YORK STATE EDUCATION DEPARTMENT, 449 F. 2d 871 (2d Cir. 1971), *vacated*, 409 U.S. 75 (1972)

*Facts:* New York enacted a statute providing for state financial assistance ($10 per pupil) for the purchase of textbooks for grades seven through twelve. The statute also enabled qualified voters within a school district to vote a tax for textbooks for grades one through six. If the voters failed to approve a proposed property tax to finance school operations, textbooks could be obtained in grades one through six only upon the payment of a rental fee ($7.50 per pupil). Indigent mothers of minor children brought an action claiming the statute to be unconstitutional. The court of appeals upheld the constitutionality of the statute, finding that the legislature's intention to promote education in certain fields by purchasing textbooks to be loaned free to grades seven through twelve, but not grades one through six, was based on a constitutionally reasonable classification. While appeal to the Court was pending, voters in the indigent mothers' school district agreed to levy a tax for the purchase of textbooks also to be loaned free to grades one through six.

*Holding:* (8/1x0) Since the voters in the school district voted to levy taxes for textbooks to be loaned free to grades one through six as permitted by statute, a claim by the indigent mothers that the statute constituted a discriminatory burden might not present a case or controversy. The case is sent back to the district court to determine whether it had become moot.

*Basis:* Courts will decline to decide arguments based on moot issues, i.e., cases no longer presenting live controversies.

## DEFUNIS v. ODEGAARD, 82 Wash. 2d. 11 507 (1973), *vacated*, 416 U.S. 312 (1974)

*Facts:* After being denied admission to a state-operated law school, DeFunis brought suit for himself alone, and not for a class of applicants, asking that the school's admission policies be declared racially discriminatory and that he be admitted to the school. The student was admitted under court order, and while appeal of that decision was pending, completed all but the final quarter. The school assured that he would be permitted to complete this final term.

*Holding:* (7x2) Since the student would be allowed to complete law school regardless of any decision on the merits of the case, there is no present controversy and the case is no longer a proper vehicle for judicial decision-making.

*Basis:* Article III of the U.S. Constitution requires that the courts decide active controversies. Since the issues raised in the case are likely to reach the Court again and since this student's opportunity to complete school is assured, the usual rule in federal cases that an actual controversy must exist at the time of review as well as at the legal action's beginning is followed here. This case is moot.

## MERCER v. MICHIGAN STATE BOARD OF EDUCATION, 379F. Supp. 580 (E. D. Michigan 1974), *aff'd,* 419 U.S. 1081 (1974)

*Facts:* A Michigan statute prohibited the giving of instruction, advice, or information on the subject of birth control by any person in the course of sex and health education classes in the public schools. In addition, parents were also permitted to exclude their children from such classes. .No person had yet been charged with breach of the statutes. A teacher in the Detroit public schools and a local physician sought to have the statutes declared unconstitutional on their face rather than as applied in any particular instance.

*Decision:* Summarily affirmed (6/3x0)

*Holding:* (of the three-judge lower court): (1) The doctor has no standing to challenge these statutes in federal court. (2) The teacher has standing to challenge the statutes, but only with regard to how they adversely affect his/her interest and not the interest of other persons, e.g., students or parents. (3) The state's elimination of birth control instruction from the public school curriculum is constitutional.

*Bases:* In order to have standing in federal courts to raise an issue concerning an alleged violation of a constitutional right, a person must first be able to show an actual interest harmed or threatened by the challenged action or statute. The challenger must have a personal stake in the outcome of the controversy such as to insure that concrete adverseness will sharpen the presentation of issues, and the injury claimed or threatened must be to an interest arguably protected by a federal statute or a constitutional provision. (1) The doctor has no standing since he cannot show an injury giving him sufficient interest in the matter. His status as a doctor does not have a sufficient relation to the statutes under attack to qualify him to challenge them in federal court. (2) The teacher has standing to challenge the statutes as they affect his status as a teacher (and if the case is properly certified as a class action, the status of other teachers), but he cannot challenge the statutes for their effect on the rights of others, who if they so wish are able to bring a challenge of their own. (3) The statutes are not overly broad so as to be violative of the First Amendment freedom of speech guaranty nor supportive of religion so as to be violative of the First Amendment establishment clause. The states have the power to establish public school curricula and to permit parents the right to determine which courses their children will attend.

## BOARD OF SCHOOL COMMISSIONERS v. JACOBS, 490 F. 2d 601 (1973), *vacated*, 420 U.S. 128 (1975)

*Facts:*  Six students who were involved in the publication and distribution of a student newspaper successfully challenged certain actions taken by the school board and other school officials which threatened to impair the students' freedom to publish and distribute the newspaper. However, the students failed to define properly in their pleadings a class of persons adversely affected by the challenged rules. In this case, the school board challenged the court rulings against certain of its rules and actions. The students have all graduated from the school system.

*Holding:*  (8x1) Since the class of students adversely affected by the school board's actions was not properly defined, there was no "class action." Therefore when the six students graduated, their case ceased to have validity as a controversy. The students are no longer adversely affected by school board action and, therefore, have no right to challenge it. The lower court decisions protecting the students have no present validity as to anyone and are void.

*Basis:*  Federal Rule of Civil Procedure 23 (c) (1) and 23 (c) (3) requires that class actions be properly certified and that the class be

117

properly identified, especially when the original complainants are not likely to be actively involved in the controversy by the time the case is appealed.

## CITIZENS FOR PARENTAL RIGHTS v. SAN MATEO COUNTY BOARD OF EDUCATION, 51 Cal. app. 3d (1975), *dismissed,* 425 U.S. 908 (1976), *reh. denied,* 425 U.S. 1000 (1976)

*Facts:* Five California public school districts instituted family life and sex education programs for public school students. The programs did not promote any particular religious viewpoint in their curricular coverage. The programs were operated in compliance with two state statutes which required that parents have both advance notice that such courses would be offered and an opportunity to preview any written or audiovisual materials to be used in them. The statutes provided parents with the right to have their children excused from the programs or from any portion of them which were offensive to the parents' religious beliefs. The three-judge federal court on a vote of 2x1 held that family life and sex education courses, which do not promote a particular religious viewpoint and which provide parents objecting to the programs with an opportunity to withdraw their children from them, are constitutional. Appeal was sought here.

*Holding:* (9x0) Where the Court does not find a "substantial federal question," e.g., violation of a federal constitutional provision, presented, it will not further review the case. Thus, the Court dismissed the case.

*Basis:* Under Article III of the Constitution, the judicial power of federal courts includes cases involving "federal questions," i.e. those involving federal statutes, treaties, or the Constitution. A case which does not fit into this or any other of the specific categories enumerated in Article III, e.g., controversies between citizens of different states, falls beyond the jurisdiction of the federal courts. The Court, therefore, cannot make a final decision in such cases. Furthermore, the federal question must be a substantal one.

118

# GLOSSARY

**Ad valorem:**   "According to the value;" a tax or duty assessed in proportion to the value of the property.

**Appellant:**   Party, be s/he plaintive or defendant at the lower court level, who upon losing at the lower level brings an appeal.

**Appellee:**   Party, be s/he plaintive or defendant at the lower court level, who is put in the position of defending the decision upon its appeal. It should be noted that the same party may become "appellant" and "appellee" at successive stages of the litigation.

**Certiorari:**   "To be made certain of;" the name of a writ of review for a case falling in the discretionary area of the Supreme Court's appellate jurisdiction, requiring an affirmative vote of four Justices.

**Class Action:**   An action brought on behalf of other persons similarly situated.

**Concurrence:**   An opinion separate from that of the majority filed by one or more Justices who agree(s) with the general result of the majority decision, but who choose(s) to emphasize or differentiate the reasoning or grounds for the decision.

**De facto:**   "In fact;" actually occurring.

**De jure:**   "By law;" occurring as a result of official action.

**Dissent:**   An opinion which disagrees with that of the majority and is handed down by one or more members of the Court.

| | |
|---|---|
| **Dismissal:** | Decision without opinion by the United States Supreme Court in the mandatory area of its appellate jurisdiction which summarily disposes of the case because of the procedural status of the parties or the issues e.g., mootness, standing, or lack of substantial federal question. |
| **Due process:** | The regular course of administration of justice through the rules and forms which have been established for the protection of private rights in courts of law. |
| **Enjoin:** | To require a person by an injunction to perform or to abstain from performing some act. |
| **Ex post facto:** | "After the fact;" a law passed after the occurrence of an act which retrospectively changes the legal consequences of the act. |
| **Ex rel:** | "Upon information of;" legal proceeding which is instituted by the Attorney General or other appropriate official in the name of and on behalf of the state, but on the information and the instigation of an individual who has a private interest in the matter. |
| **In loco parentis:** | "In place of parents;" charged with a parent's rights, duties and responsibility. In the case of a teacher, this is a condition applying only when the child is under the reasonable control and supervision of the school. |
| **In re:** | "In the matter of;" designating a judicial proceeding, e.g., juvenile cases, in which the customary adversarial posture of the parties is deemphasized or nonexistent. |
| **Incorporation:** | Evolving doctrine by which the United States Supreme Court has applied a substantial part of the Bill of Rights, e.g., First Amendment, to the states and thereby public school officials via the Fourteenth Amendment. |
| **Infra:** | "Below;" cross reference to a fuller citation appearing subsequently in the document. |

| | |
|---|---|
| **Inter alia:** | "Among other things." |
| **One-judge opinion in chambers:** | Special ruling issued by a Supreme Court Justice under unusual circumstances and thus not carrying full precedential effect. |
| **Moot:** | An issue which is not considered by the Court because it no longer contains a live dispute of the sort proper for a judicial decision. A moot case seeks to determine an abstract question which does not arise upon facts or rights existing at the time. |
| **Parens patriae:** | "Parent of the country;" referring to the states as having sovereign power of guardianship over persons under a disability, such as minors and insane persons. |
| **Per Curiam:** | "By the Court;" an opinion concurred in by several/or all the members of the Court but without disclosing the name of any particular Justice as being its author. |
| **Police power of state:** | The power vested in the legislature to make and establish laws, statutes, and ordinances which would be for the good of the state and its people. This power extends to all areas of health, morals, safety, order, and comfort of the people. |
| **Prima facie:** | "On first appearance" or "on its face;" evidence which is presumed to be true unless rebutted by proof to the contrary. |
| **Remand:** | "To send back;" action by an appellate court to send the case back to a lower court for further proceedings. |
| **Standing:** | Status as a proper party before the Court as determined by the Court; requires an actual injury or immediate interest in the action at hand. |
| **Statute:** | A law enacted by the legislative branch of the federal or state government. |
| **Sub nom:** | "Under the name of;" designation for the change in the |

name of either party (or both parties) in the course of the litigation, e.g., upon the death of one of the parties during the appellate process.

**Supra:** "Above;" cross reference to a fuller citation appearing earlier in the document.

**Summary affirmance:** Decision without an opinion by the United States Supreme Court in the mandatory area of its appellate jurisdiction which gives binding effect to the lower court's decision* but which does not have as much precedential value as a full opinion by the Court on the merits.** Thus, the Court feels less constrained to overrule summary affirmances than full opinions while it expects lower courts to follow both equally. The jurisdictional statement filed in the parties' briefs to the Court, rather than the lower court opinion, must be the focus of any inquiry regarding the scope and meaning of the summary affirmance.***

**U.S. Reports:** Official reports of the United States Supreme Court decisions, as contrasted to parallel citations of unofficial reports of the decisions which are available through Shephard's and other such reference volumes.

**Void for vagueness:** Constitutional infirmity when a law is so unclear that it does not provide the specificity required by due process, thus making it void.

---

* *Hicks v. Miranda*, 422 U.S. 322, 345 (1976) (summary dismissal). The *Hicks* rule was applied to summary affirmances in *Doe v. Hodgson*, 500 F. 2d 1206, 1207-08 (2d. Cir. 1974); *Virgin Islands v. 19,623 Acres of Land*, 536 F. 2d 566, 571 (3d. Cir. 1976); *Thonen v. Jenkins*, 517 F. 2d 3, 7 (4th Cir. 1975); *Whitlow v. Hodges*, 539 F. 2d 582, 584 (6th Cir. 1976); *Bemid v. Stanton*, 528 F. 2d 688, 691 (7th Cir. 1976); *Brady v. State Bar of California*, 533 F. 2d 502, 503n. 1 (9th Cir. 1976).

** *Hicks v. Miranda*, 422 U.S. 322, 345n. 1 (1976); *McCarthy v. Philadelphia Civil Service Comm'n (supra)*.

*** *Edelman v. Jordan*, 415 U.S. 651, 671 (1976)

# TABLE OF CASES

The principal cases are in italic type. Other cases cited are in roman type. References are to pages.

*Abington School District v. Schempp,* 19
*Abood v. Detroit Board of Education,* 72
*Adler v. Board of Education,* 52
*Alexander v. Holmes County Board of Education,* 87
*Arlington Heights v. Metropolitan Housing Development Corp.,* 106
*Askew v. Hargrave,* 12
*Atchison Board of Education v. DeKay,* 4
*Attorney General of Michigan ex rel. Kies v. Lowrey,* 6
Austin Independent School District v. United States, 104

*Baggett v. Bullitt,* 57
*Baker v. Owen,* 45
*Bartels v. Iowa,* 49
*Beilan v. Board of Public Education,* 54
Bemid v. Stanton, 122
*Bishop v. Wood,* 66
*Board of Education v. Allen,* 20
*Board of Regents v. Roth,* 63
*Board of School Commissioners v. Jacobs,* 117
*Bolling v. Sharpe,* 81
*Bradley v. School Board ("Bradley I"),* 84
*Bradley v. School Board ("Bradley II"),* 100
Brady v. State Bar of California, 122
*Brown v. Board of Education ("Brown I"),* 80
*Brown v. Board of Education ("Brown II"),* 81

*Carter v. West Feliciana Parish School Board,* 88
*Chamberlin v. Dade County Board of Public Instruction,* 20
*Citizens for Parental Rights v. San Mateo County Board of Education,* 118
*Cleveland Board of Education v. LaFleur,* 98
*Cochran v. Louisiana State Board of Education,* 16
*Codd v. Velger,* 71
*Cohen v. Chesterfield School Board,* 98
*Cole v. Richardson,* 62
*Committee for Public Education and Religious Liberty v. Nyquist,* 26

123

*Connell v. Higginbotham*, 62
*Cooper v. Aaron*, 82
*Cramp v. Board of Public Instruction*, 56
*Cumming v. Richmond County Board of Education*, 77

*Davis v. Board of School Commissioners*, 91
*Davis v. Indiana*, 3
*Dayton Board of Education v. Brinkman*, 110
*DeFunis v. Odegaard*, 115
*Dodge v. Board of Education*, 50
Doe v. Hodgson, 122
*Doon v. Cummins*, 3
*Doremus v. Board of Education*, 113
*Dowell v. Board of Education*, 87
*Drummond v. Acree*, 95

*Earley v. Dicenso*, 21
Edelman v. Jordan, 122
*Elfbrandt v. Russell*, 58
*Ellis v. Dixon*, 113
*Engel v. Vitale*, 19
*Epperson v. Arkansas*, 61
*Evans v. Buchanan*, 103
*Everson v. Board of Education*, 17

*Farrington v. Tokushige*, 77
*Flast v. Cohen*, 114

*Garner v. Board of Public Works*, 51
*Gault, In re*, 37
*Geduldig v. Aiello*, 65
*Gilmore v. Montgomery*, 101
*Gong Lum v. Rice*, 78
*Gordon v. Lance*, 13
*Goss v. Board of Education*, 82
*Goss v. Lopez*, 42
*Grayned v. City of Rockford*, 39
*Green v. County School Board*, 85
*Griffin v. County School Board*, 83
*Griggs v. Duke Power Co.*, 88

*Guey Hung Lee v. Johnson, 92*

*Hadley v. Junior College District, 11*
*Hazlewood School District v. United States, 109*
*Healy v. James, 41*
Hicks v. Miranda, 122

*Hortonville Joint School District No. 1 v. Hortonville Education Association, 67*
Hunt v. McNair, 29

*Illinois ex rel. McCollum v. Board of Education, 18*
*Indiana ex rel. Anderson v. Brand, 50*
*Indiana ex. rel. Stanton v. Glover, 5*
*Ingraham v. Wright, 46*
*International Brotherhood of Teamsters v. United States, 72*

*Jacobson v. Massachusetts, 33*
*Jefferson Parish School Board v. Dandridge, 93*
*Johnson v. New York State Education Department, 115*
*Johnson v. Sanders, 23*

*Keyes v. School District No. 1, Denver, Colorado, 96*
*Keyishian v. Board of Regents, 58*
*Kramer v. Union Free School District No. 15, 9*

*Lau v. Nichols, 98*
*Lemon v. Kurtzman ("Lemon I"), 21*
*Lemon v. Kurtzman ("Lemon II"), 24*
*Lerner v. Casey, 55*
*Levitt v. Commission for Public Education and Religious Liberty, 25*

*McCarthy v. Philadelphia Civil Service Commission, 66*
*McDaniel v. Barresi, 92*
*McInnis v. Ogilvie, 9*
*McLaurin v. Oklahoma State Regents for Higher Education, 79*
*Madison v. Wisconsin Employment Relations Commission, 69*
*Maryland v. Wirtz, 60*
*Massachussetts Board of Retirement v. Murgia, 68*
*Mayor of Philadelphia v. Educational Equality League, 99*

*Meek v. Pittenger*, 28
*Mercer v. Michigan State Board of Education*, 116
Metropolitan School District v. Buckley, 106
*Meyer v. Nebraska*, 48
*Milliken v. Bradley ("Milliken I")*, 102
*Milliken v. Bradley ("Milliken II")*, 108
*Minersville School District v. Gobitis*, 35
*Monroe v. Board of Commissoners*, 85
*Montana ex. rel. Haire v. Rice*, 7
*Mount Healthy City School District v. Doyle*, 70
*Murray v. Curlett*, 19

*National League of Cities v. Usery*, 68
*New Orleans v. Fisher*, 6
*Norwood v. Harrison*, 97

*Papish v. Board of Carators*, 42
*Pasadena City Board of Education v. Spangler*, 105
Paul v. Davis, 64
*Perry v. Sindermann*, 64
*Phelps v. Board of Education*, 49
*Pickering v. Board of Education*, 60
*Pierce v. Society of Sisters*, 16
*Plessy v. Ferguson*, 76
*Police Department v. Mosley*, 38

*Roemer v. Board of Public Works*, 29
*Rogers v. Paul*, 84
*Runyon v. McCrary*, 105

*Sailors v. Board of Education*, 8
*San Antonio Independent School District v. Rodriguez*, 13
*Shelton v. Tucker*, 56
Singleton v. Jackson Municipal Separate School District, 88
*Sloan v. Lemon*, 27
*Slochower v. Board of Higher Education*, 54
*Spencer v. Kugler*, 93
*Springfield v. Quick*, 2
*Swann v. Charlotte-Mecklenburg Board of Education*, 90
*Sweatt v. Painter*, 79

*Taylor v. Mississippi, 36*
Thonen v. Jenkins, 122
Tilton v. Richardson, 29
*Tinker v. Des Moines Independent Community School District, 38*
*Turner v. Fouche, 10*

United Airlines v. McMann, 68
*United States v. Montgomery County Board of Education, 86*
*United States v. Scotland Neck City Board of Education, 95*

Virgin Islands v. 19,623 Acres of Land, 122
*Vorcheimer v. School District of Philadelphia, 107*

*Walz v. Tax Commission, 21*
*Washington v. Davis, 104*
*Waugh v. Board of Trustees, 34*
*West Virginia State Board of Education v. Barnette, 36*
*Wheeler v. Barrera, 27*
*Whitehill v. Elkins, 59*
Whitlow v. Hodges, 122
*Wieman v. Updegraff, 53*
*Williams v. McNair, 89*
*Wisconsin v. Yoder, 24*
*Wolman v. Walter, 30*
*Wood v. Strickland, 43*
*Wright v. Council of City of Emporia, 94*

*Zorach v. Clauson, 18*
*Zucht v. King, 35*

# Index

Academic freedom, 56, 58-59
Age discrimination, 68-69
Alabama, 91, 101-102
Amish, 24
Aptitude tests, 88-89, 104
Arizona, 58, 85-86
Arkansas, 56, 61, 82
Arm bands, 33, 38
Article I: Commerce, viii, 60-61; General
    Welfare, vii; Impairment of Contracts,
    viii, 6-7, 50-51
Article III, 106, 113, 114-115, 116, 118
Article IV, 7
Article VI, 82
Assembly, freedom of; See Freedom of
    Assembly
Association, freedom of; See Freedom of
    Association
Bible reading, 15, 19-20, 113
Bills of Attainder, 52
Bonds: liability employment, 4-6; state
    limits, 3-4, 7-8, 9; validity, 3-5; voter
    ratification, 2, 13
Busing, 75, 90-92, 95-96
California, 51-52, 65, 92-93, 98, 105-106,
    118
California Education Code, 92
Chinese, 78-79, 92-93, 98
Civil Rights Act of 1964: aptitude tests,
    88-89, 104; busing, 92; compensatory
    education, 98; desegregation, 106;
    hiring, 72-73, 88-89, 104, 109-110;
    promotion, 73, 88-89; seniority sys-
    tem, 73
Class action, 106, 112, 117-118, 119
Collective bargaining, 48, 69-70, 72
College; See Higher education
Colorado, 96-97

Communist activities, 53-55, 56-58. See
    also Proscribed organizations
Compelling state interest, 10, 103
Compensatory education, 98, 108-109
Compulsory attendance: Amish, 24; public
    schools, 16
Connecticut, 23, 41
Constitution; See specific Articles,
    Amendments, and freedoms
Contracts: employment, 64; private
    schools, 105, racial discrimination, 105,
    religious schools, 25; retirement an-
    nuities, 50; school district boundaries,
    7; tenure, 49-50, 51, 64-65
Corporal punishment, 33, 45-46
Creditors, 3-6
Cruel and unusual punishment, viii, 46. See
    also Corporal punishment
Delaware, 80, 103
Desegregation, 74-76; attendance zones,
    82-83, 87-88, 90-91, 92-93, 102-103,
    110-111; busing, 75, 90-92, 95-96;
    Chinese, 92-93; closing public schools,
    83; delay of implementation, 81-82, 87-
    88, 92-93, 94, 100-101; free transfer
    plans, 82-83, 85-86, 90; freedom of
    choice plans, 74-75, 85, 95; grade-a-
    year plans, 84; neighborhood school
    concept, 91; non-racial faculty assign-
    ment, 84, 86-87, 90; public recreational
    facilities, 101-102; racial balance, 75,
    86, 90, 92, 93, 96, 105-106, 110-111;
    reimbursement of legal fees, 100-101;
    remedial education costs, 108-109;
    school districts, 76, 93, 94-95, 96-97,
    102-103. See also Racial Discrimina-
    tion; Segregation

Discrimination: compensatory education, 98; educational funding, 1-2, 9, 12, 13-14; federal aid, 98; school district elections, 9-10, 11-12; school facilities, 113-114; supplying textbooks, 115. *See also* Age discrimination; Desegregation; Minority Groups; Racial discrimination; Segregation; Sex discrimination

Dismissal, employee; *See* Public employees, dismissal

District of Columbia, 81, 104

Due process, 32-33; compulsory attendance, 16; constitutional clause, ix; contracts, 50; definition, 120; educational funding, 9; employee dismissal, 52, 53-54, 62, 63, 67; expulsion, 44; foreign language teaching, 48; fraternities, 34; hearings, 62, 63; juvenile courts, 33, 38; loyalty oaths, 52, 53, 59, 62, 63; maternity leave, 99; noise ordinances, 40; perjury, 59; racial discrimination, 104; right to teach, 48; state aid to religious schools, 17; suspension, 43. *See also* Liberty interest; Property interest

E.S.E.A., 27-28, 114-115

Eighth Amendment, viii, 46

Eleventh Amendment, ix, 109

Employees; *See* Public employees

Equal Educational Opportunity Act of 1974, 108

Equal protection: age classification, 68-69; compensatory education, 98; constitutional clause, ix; desegregation, 80-88, 91-95, 97, 102-103; educational funding, 1, 2, 9, 12, 14; fraternities, 34; housing, 106-107; picketing, 39; public office, 10-11; public recreational facilities, 102; pregnancy disability, 65; retirement, 68-69; salary reductions, 50; segregation, 77, 79, 80, 81, 97-98; single-sex schools, 90, 108; state aid to segregated schools, 83, 97-98; voting, 11-12, 13

Establishment of religion: bible reading, 15, 19-20; constitutional clause, viii;

evolution, 61; higher education, 30; prayer, 15, 19-20; released time, 19; religious instruction in public schools, 18; sex education, 117; state aid to religious schools, 15, 18, 21, 22-23, 25-31, 114-115. *See also* Free exercise of religion; Religious instruction; Religious schools, state aid to

Evolution, 15, 47, 61

*Ex post facto* laws, 52, 120

Exclusive access, 101-102

Expression, freedom of; *See* Freedom of speech

Expulsion, 36-37, 43-44

Fair Housing Act of 1968, 106

Fair Labor Standards Act, 60-61, 68

Federal Rule of Civil Procedure, 117-118

Fee Award Law, 100-101

Fifth Amendment: due process, viii, 81, 104; liberty interest, 78; property interest, 78; self-incrimination, viii, 37-38, 54, 55

Financing of Education; *See* Bonds; Creditors; Per-Pupil expenditures; Religious schools, state aid to

First Amendment; *See* Establishment of religion; Free exercise of religion; Freedom of assembly; Freedom of association; Freedom of speech; Freedom of the press

Flag salute, 16, 32, 33-35

Florida, 12, 20, 46, 56-57, 62

Foreign language teaching, 47, 48, 77-78

Fourteenth Amendment: desegregation, 106, 109, 111; employee rights, 47-48; school board appointments, 100; segregation, 77, 79; student rights, 32-33; voting rights, 8. *See also* Due process; Equal protection; Incorporation; Liberty interest; Property interest; Void for vagueness

Fraternities, 32, 34

Free exercise of religion: Amish 24; compulsory attendance, 24; constitutional clause, viii; flag salute, 16, 35-36; Jehovah's Witnesses, 36; released time, 18-19. *See also* Establishment

of religion; Religious instruction; Religious schools, state aid to
Freedom of assembly: constitutional clause, viii; proscribed organizations, 53
Freedom of association: campus organizations, 33, 41; investigations of employee fitness, 55, 56; loyalty oaths, 53, 58-59, 62-63; proscribed organizations, 56, 58-59; segregated groups, 102
Freedom of religion; See Free exercise of religion
Freedom of speech: arm bands, 33, 38; constitutional clause, viii; flag salute, 32, 35-37; investigations of employee fitness, 55; loyalty oaths, 58, 59, 62, 63; minimum education, 14; picketing, 33, 39-40; proscribed organization, 53; public statements, 60, 65, 69-71; noise ordinances, 40; sex education, 117; student newspapers, 42; union dues, 72
Freedom of the press, 33, 42
Georgia, 10-11, 92, 95-96
H.E.W. guidelines, 98
Hawaii, 77-78
Hearings: Corporal punishment, 33, 46; employee dismissal, 52-53, 54-55, 56, 60, 62-65, 66-67, 71; juvenile courts, 37-38; suspension, 33, 42-43
Higher education: admissions discrimination, 115-116; campus organizations, 41; employee dismissal, 54, 63-65; fraternities, 34; junior college districts, 11-12; loyalty oaths, 53, 57-58, 58-59; proscribed organizations, 53, 57-58, 58-59; segregation, 79-80; single-sex schools, 89-90; state aid, 29-30; student newspapers, 42
Hispano-Americans, 76, 96-97
Housing, 106-107
Illinois, 9, 18, 38-40, 60
Immunity from suit, 33, 44
Incarceration, 37-38
Incorporation: definition, 120; First Amendment rights, 15, 18, 20, 29, 36, 37, 38, 41, 56, 61, 65, 71

Indiana, 2-3, 5-6, 50-51
Interstate commerce, 60-61
Interstate travel, 66
Iowa, 3-4, 38, 49
Japanese, 77-78
Jehovah's Witnesses, 36
Jurisdiction of federal courts, 12, 81, 112, 113-114, 118. See also Article III
Jury selection, 10-11
Juvenile courts, 37-38
Kansas, 4-5, 80
Land grants; See Public lands
Liberty interests: corporal punishment, 33, 45, 46; employee dismissal, 63-64, 67, 71; foreign language teaching, 49, 78; hearings, 71; juvenile courts, 38; parents, 16, 45, 78; police power, 34; pregnancy leave, 99; reputation, 43, 63-64, 67, 71; suspension, 43; vaccination, 33-34
Louisiana, 6, 16-17, 76-77
Low income groups, 26-28, 65, 106-107
Loyalty oaths, 47, 51-52, 53, 56-59, 62-63
Maryland, 29-30, 59, 60-61
Massachusetts, 33-34, 62-63, 68-69
Michigan, 6-7, 8, 72, 102-103, 108-109, 116-117
Minority groups: Amish, 24; Chinese, 78-79; 92-93, 98; elderly, 68-69; Hispano-Americans, 76, 96-97; Japanese, 77-78; Jehovah's Witnesses, 36; low-income groups, 13-14, 26, 27-28, 65, 106-107. See also Discrimination; Desegregation; Racial discrimination; Segregation
Mississippi, 36, 78-79, 87, 97-98
Missouri, 11-12, 27-28, 42, 109-110
Montana, 7-8
Mootness, 106, 112, 115, 116, 121
Nebraska, 48
Neighborhood school concept, 91
New Jersey, 17-18, 49-50, 93, 113
New York, 9-10, 18-19, 20-21, 25-27, 52-53, 54, 55, 58-59, 115
New York City charter, 54
Newspapers; See Student newspapers
Noise ordinances, 40

North Carolina, 45, 90-91
Ohio, 30-31, 42-43, 49, 98-99, 110-111
Oklahoma, 53, 79-80
Oregon, 16
*Parens Patriae,* 24, 121
Parents' rights, 16, 45, 49, 78
Parochial schools; *See* Religious schools, state aid to
Pennsylvania, 19-20, 21-23, 24-25, 27, 28-29, 35-36, 54-55, 66, 99-100, 107-108
Per-pupil expenditures, 2, 9, 12, 13-14
Perjury, 58, 59-60
Picketing, 33, 38-40
Police power of state, 34, 35, 51, 121
Prayer, 15, 19-20
Pregnancy disability, 65, 98-99
Private schools: admissions discrimination, 105; foreign language teaching, 49, 77-78; higher education, 29-30; property interest, 16, 78; segregation, 83, 97-98, 105; state aid, 29-30, 83, 97-98. *See also* Religious schools, state aid to
Property interest: employment, 63-65, 67; private schools, 16, 78; school district boundaries, 1, 7; student's education, 33, 43
Proscribed organizations, 51-53, 56, 57-59
Public employees, 47-48; classification, 49-50; contracts, 50-51; dismissals, 51-57, 58-59, 60, 62-65, 66-67, 70-71; hours, 60-61, 68; minimum wages, 60-61, 68; residency requirements, 48, 66; retirement, 48, 50, 68-69; salary reductions, 49-50
Public lands, 2-3, 7-8
Public office, 1-2, 10-11
Racial discrimination, 74-76; aptitude tests, 88-89, 104; contracts, 105; hiring, 72-73, 88-89, 104, 109-110; housing, 106-107; job promotions, 72-73, 88-89; jury selection, 10-11; religious reasons, 105; school admissions, 105, 115-116; school boards, 10-11, 99-100; seniority system, 72-73; teacher assignments, 84, 86-87, 90, 109-110. *See also* Desegregation; Segregation

Religion; *See* Establishment of religion; Free exercise of religion; Religious instruction; Religious schools, state aid to
Religious instruction: Bible reading, 15, 19-20, 113; evolution, 15, 47, 61; prayer, 15, 19-20; public schools, 18; released time, 15, 18-19; sex education, 118
Religious schools, state aid to: contracts, 24-25; facility maintenance, 26-27; federal funds, 27-28, 114-115; higher education, 29-30; instructional materials, 22, 28-29, 30-31; personnel, 28-29; remedial services, 28-29, 30-31; salaries, 15, 22-23; tax credits, 16, 26-27; tax exemptions, 21; test administration, 25-26, 30-31; textbooks, 15, 16-17, 20-21, 22-23, 28-29, 30-31; transportation, 15, 17-18, 30-31; tuition reimbursement, 15-16, 26-27
Remedial education; *See* Compensatory education
Reputation, 43, 63-64, 66-67, 71
Residency requirements, 48, 66
Retirement, 48, 50, 68-69
Rhode Island, 21-22
SDS, 41
School boards: elections, 8, 9 10; liability for bonds, 4-6; membership requirements, 10-11; racial imbalance, 10-11, 99-100
School districts: boundaries, 1, 6-7, 93; desegregation, 93, 94-95, 96-97, 102-103; elections, 9-12; funds, 13-14; junior college, 11-12; tax variations, 9, 12, 13-14
School finance; *See* Bonds; Creditors; Per-pupil expenditures; Religious schools, state aid to
Sectarian schools; *See* Religious schools, state aid to
Security laws, 55
Segregation, 74-76; Chinese, 78-79; high school, 77; higher education, 79-80; private schools, 83, 97-98, 105; railways, 76-77; violation of constitution, 80-81. *See also* Desegregation;

131

Racial discrimination
Self-incrimination; *See* Fifth Amendment, self-incrimination
Seniority system, 73
Separate but equal; *See* Segregation
Separation of church and state; *See* Establishment of religion
Sex discrimination, 74, 76; pregnancy disability, 65, 98-99; single-sex schools, 89-90, 107-108
Sex education, 116-117, 118
Slavery; *See* Thirteenth Amendment
South Carolina, 80, 89-90
Speech, freedom of; *See* Freedom of speech
Standing, 112, 114-115, 116-117, 121
States' rights; *See* Tenth amendment
Strikes, 67
Student newspapers, 42, 117
Subversive organizations; *See* Proscribed organizations
Suspension, 33, 38, 42-43
Taxes: accounting, 6; *ad valorem,* 12, 119; collection, 1, 2, 6; Congress, 114; credits, 26-27; distribution, 1, 2-3; exemptions, 21; school district variations, 1, 2, 9, 12, 13-14; state limits, 9, 12; supplying textbooks, 16-17, 115; voter ratification, 13, 115
Teachers; *See* Public employees
Teamsters' Union, 72-73
Tennessee, 82-83
Tenth Amendment, viii, 61, 68, 109
Tenure, 47, 49-50, 51, 54, 64-65
Texas, 13-14, 35, 64-65, 79
Thirteenth Amendment, ix, 77, 105
Title VIII, section 803, 95-96
Title 42 U.S.C., 43-44, 105
Treasonable acts, 58
Union dues, 72
Vaccination, 33-34, 35
Virginia, 80, 83, 85, 98-99
Void for vagueness: definition, 122, loyalty oaths; 47-48, 56-58; picketing, 39, 40; proscribed organizations, 52-53, 56-58
Voting: 60% rule, 2, 13; eligibility, 1-2, 9-10; school board elections, 8; school district elections, 1-2, 9-10, 11-12; taxes, 13, 115
Washington, 57-58
West Virginia, 13, 36-37
Wisconsin, 24, 63-64, 67, 69-70